KLONDIKE GOLD RUSH
CENTENNIAL 1897-1997

Klondike Gold Rush Centennial Anthology

KLONDIKE GOLD RUSH
CENTENNIAL

KLONDIKE GOLD RUSH
CENTENNIAL COMMITTEE
of WASHINGTON STATE

A Project of the Greater Seattle
Chamber of Commerce
1301 Fifth Avenue, Suite 2400
Seattle, Washington 98101
(206) 389-7240

Klondike Gold Rush Centennial Anthology iii

Members of the Literary Contest Committee
Jack R. Evans, Chairman
Deborah K. Daoust
Neile Graham
Robert Sheldon

Graphic Design and Formatting for publication: Michael Jaynes
Printer: Data Reproductions Corporation

For information write to
Klondike Gold Rush Centennial Committee of Washington State,
1301 Fifth Avenue, Suite 2400, Seattle, WA 98101
Phone (206) 389-7240

Library of Congress Catalog Card No. 97-073941

ISBN 1-877882-22-4

Klondike Gold Rush Centennial Anthology

Acknowledgments

Planning for the centennial celebration of the Klondike Gold Rush was started two years ago by a small group of people headed by Reed W. Jarvis with the encouragement of Ralph Munro, Washington Secretary of State. The core group who remained active during the long gestation period included Robert Brown, Jack R. Evans, Leone Ewoldt, and Denise Jarvis. This group organized the Klondike Gold Rush Centennial Committee of Washington State to coordinate and monitor the events of the three year celebration. Its members then began meeting with representatives of similar groups in Alaska, the Yukon Territory and British Columbia to coordinate activities and events being held in Seattle, Alaska and the Yukon Territory. In January 1997 this committee came under the sponsorship and support of the Greater Seattle Chamber of Commerce, whose activities a hundred years ago helped to put Seattle on the map. We appreciate and acknowledge their support.

The committee is indebted to those individual and corporate sponsors listed or profiled in the back pages of this publication. They gave the dollars needed to publish this anthology.

The Board of Directors gave generously of their time and ideas and butted their heads together for the past two years. They showed up for meetings and events when they might have preferred to stay at their desks or go fishing.

Many people helped to plan and carry out the centennial events and the literary contest. We want to single out some of them for special recognition. We could not have done anything without the untiring administrative assistance of Kristi James and her prompt response to our many requests for help. Mike Jaynes applied his admirable skill in design and layout in preparing the material for publication. We owe a note of thanks to our fine printer, Data Reproductions Corporation. We love Denise Jarvis for her generous support throughout the early stages of planning for the Centennial celebration. She provided research and admonishment. We can never forget Reed Jarvis who believed in the impossible and did the impossible, and whose generosity of spirit never flagged. Kay Boyd graciously permitted the use of reproductions of her art work from the "Friendship Quilt" commemorating the 58th Sourdough Reunion of 1990. Our thanks to Ian and Sally Wilson for the contribution of their book *Gold Rush, North to Alaska and the Klondike* as a prize. We are grateful to all the literary contest participants for having the courage to submit their creative efforts. We are indebted to the judges: Linda Bierds, Howard Clifford, and the late Charles Lillard, who read eighty-two poems, twenty-two stories, and seven pieces of creative nonfiction, and then brought to bear their considerable literary talents in choosing the winning entries.

In memory of Charles Lillard
1944-1997

Contents

Klondike Gold Rush Centennial
Committee of Washington State
Board of Directors

Charles Riley, President/Chairman
   Executive Vice-President of US Bank,
   Community Relations

Reed W. Jarvis, Community Outreach Chair
   Retired: National Park Service Historian and
   original planner for Klondike Gold Rush National
   Historical Park

Renata Benett, Vice Chair, Co-Chair, Ton of Gold Weekend
   Manager, Market Research, Totem Ocean Trailer
   Express, Inc., Seattle

Jack R. Evans, Secretary
   Publisher, SCW Publications, Seattle

Leone Ewoldt, Treasurer
   Pioneer Square Business Owner: WE Hats, Seattle

Eric Larsen
   Director of Marketing, Bay Pavilion, Pier 57, Seattle

Robert Brown
   Tourism Program Manager, Canadian Consulate
   General, Seattle

George Scott, Ph.D.
   State Archivist, State of Washington, Olympia

Michael Herschenshon, Ph.D.
   Director, The Museum of History & Industry, Seattle

Larry Swift, Ph.D.
   Executive Director, The Washington State School
   Director's Association, Olympia

John Blackman
   President, Argosy, Seattle

Shari Gross, Co-Chair, Ton of Gold Weekend
   President, Gross & Associates, Seattle

Frederick S. Richard, Co-Chair, Finance Committee
   Sr. Vice President, National Bank of Alaska, Seattle

Jim Van der Veen
> Director, Cargo Operations, Crowley Maritime
> Corporation, Seattle

Steve Isaacson, Co-Chair, Finance Committee
> Division Manager, Safeco Credit Company, Inc.,
> Seattle

Robert Backstein
> Attorney, Eisenhowser & Carl Carlson, Tacoma

Stephanie Toothman, Ph.D., Chair, Education Committee,
> Chief of Cultural Resources, National Park Service,
> Seattle

Gretchen Luxenberg, Co-Chair, Education Committee
> Historian, National Park Service, Seattle

Michael Luis, Chairman, Marketing & Promotion Committee
> Vice President, Public Affairs and Communications,
> Greater Seattle Chamber of Commerce

Dana Cox
> Public Relations Director/Asst. Manager,
> Underground Tour, Bill Speidel's

Michael Yaeger
> President, Studio Solstone

Lee McAnerney
> President, Alaska - Yukon Pioneers. Seattle

Beriah Brown

Paul McCarthy
> President & CEO, WLN

Christopher I. M. Houser, Ex-Officio Member
> Retired President, Union Bank Foundation,
> Los Angeles, California

Garry Schalliol, Ex-Officio Member
> Education Coordinator, Washington State Historical
> Society, Tacoma

Contest Judges

LINDA BIERDS has published four books of poetry, most recently *The Ghost Trio* (Henry Holt, 1994). Her awards include two grants from the National Endowment for the Arts and fellowships from the Guggenheim Memorial Foundation, the Ingram Merrill Foundation, and the Artist Trust Foundation of Washington. Her work has appeared in numerous magazines, including *The New Yorker* and *The Atlantic Monthly*. She is an associate professor of English at the University of Washington.

The late **CHARLES LILLARD**, columnist, historian, poet and writer is the author of nine collections of poetry and several original volumes of history. *His Seven Shillings a Year* is the standard history of Vancouver Island. He has also written over twenty-four books on art, travel, biography and bibliography. He has taught at the University of British Columbia, Matsqui Institute, Camosun College and the University of Victoria. He has been an editor for the Provincial Archives of British Columbia. In his earlier years he worked as a boom man and roustabout on the Northwest Coast and as a crew boss and machine operator for Environment Canada. Mr. Lillard was born in California in 1944, grew up in Southeastern Alaska and was educated in the United States, Europe and Canada (BA, MFA).

HOWARD CLIFFORD, an award-winning writer and photographer, has traveled extensively in Alaska and the Yukon. He is a former newspaperman and in times past has been a commercial airplane pilot, sports announcer, ski instructor, film producer, editor and publisher. Mr. Clifford's book, *Doing The White Pass*, the story of the White Pass & Yukon route and the Klondike Gold Rush, is in its third printing. He has also written *Skagway Story* (Alaska Northwest Books) and *Rails North* (Superior Publishing Co.).

Kay Boyd, © 1984 · Courtesy of The International Sourdough Reunion

Introduction

When the grimy ship, *Portland*, arrived in Seattle on July 17, 1897, sixty-eight miners disembarked carrying suitcases, sacks, cans, bottles, even blankets—all filled with gold. Wildly cheering well-wishers and wannabes jammed Schwabacher's dock to greet the new millionaires. It was the beginning of a frenzy of activity in which Seattle became the jumping-off point for the Klondike as businesses sprang up to accommodate the fortune seekers. The news of the gold strike in the Klondike mesmerized the world. Though they had only a vague notion of where the Klondike was, or how they would get there, men (and women) from all over the world left their homes, families and jobs to join the stampede. They were policemen and politicians, farmers and financiers, doctors and dentists, lawyers and laborers. Even poets and writers.

Few stampeders who made it to the Klondike found any gold. But those who survived the experience would never forget it. Most of them had never crossed a mountain or run the rapids of a river. They slogged through snow, mud and muck. They endured miserable living conditions. They were resourceful and courageous. They were foolhardy. They learned when it was time to quit and when to endure.

The old stories of those stampeders have been brought alive by new pens. The poetry, stories and creative nonfiction in this anthology are the winning entries of the SPECIAL KLONDIKE GOLD RUSH CENTENNIAL LITERARY CONTEST. Their publication is dedicated to the memory of those who participated in that great adventure one hundred years ago. We hope the reader will enjoy these original stories and poems that celebrate the timeless qualities of the human spirit. This connection with those men and women is the legacy that is being recognized and celebrated at this centennial of the Klondike Gold Rush.

Jack R. Evans
Literary Contest Chairman

Klondike Gold Rush Centennial Anthology xiii

Kay Boyd, © 1984 · Courtesy of The International Sourdough Reunion

Anna, washing

In 1897 Anna Malm left Finland with her husband Abe, seeking gold in Canada's Yukon. To assure steady income, Anna insisted Abe tote her washing machine over Chilkoot Pass. She eventually opened Malm's Arctic Laundry in the border town of Eagle, Alaska.

I. The S.S. Islander, nearing Dyea, Alaska, Oct-1897

From afar, their searchlight looks like twin globes,
floating both above and barely under
the water. The reflected cousin strobes
through the bow's wake. On deck, Anna wonders
if secretly the moon is swarming, not
ice-white and alone as she had supposed,
but packed with men, restless on rotted cots,
snoring and hot in foul, three-day-old clothes,
while below black nags buck a coal-fire roar
char keeps these endless rides turning. Quick gales
sweep down from the mountains as they near shore.
The south sun glows. Fast in his bunk, Abe scales
ice stairs to the moon, his year-cache carted
by comets. His gold-pans flicker with stars.

II. The Anthony Wayne Washing Machine, The Scales, Chilkoot Trail, Nov-1897

Her washer sways against the counterweight
then sinks. The packer adds another stone,
watches it drop, then lift. Abe asks the rate
per pound again. Anna rests on the bones
of a boat. Around her: forks, one left glove,
spring-mounted seats, chains, cog-wheels. A woman
stumbles, strapped to a sheet-iron stove,
rises, rejoins the man-train worming
its way to the summit Anna thinks, *If
he does this, if—this once—he would bend,
I could pull him close, let his broad hands lift
my hems, close my eyes, remember Finland...*
The packer shoves her washer from the scale.
Abe shouts, squints at the slope, reckons angle.

III. *Abe at the Ironing Board, Eagle, Alaska, 1900*

He *shucks* the plane toward the plank's nose, blows
curled shavings away. He runs his thick thumb
along the grain. Two months, he almost froze,
whipsawing this green pine—the steady thrum
of jag-teeth dwindling to a labored gnaw
and spew: a hum, dull in his cold-numbed ears.
Now, he rounds this heartwood to suit Anna,
squints to cipher sleeve-width, the way he veered
through Whitehorse Rapids, churned soap-white with silt.
They jerked like shirts inside Anna's machine.
He stretches flannel from a worn-out quilt
over the place Mounties painted his name:
this board floats, they said, *your bodies will sink.*
Anna, on shore, dunks tubs for day's washing.

IV. *Soap-Making, 1910*

All morning, Anna leached lye from alders,
simmered tallow from the broken femurs
of moose. Now she hems cuffs of Abe's trousers
to match his shrinking stride. River-steamers
blow grey plumes, unloading last supplies
before freeze-up. Ice floes—pounding like clogs—
remind her of shapes spinning in lamplight,
how they rolled back rugs in the Redmen lodge,
Abe's overshoes awkward as syllables
of stumbled English. Her thimble finger steals
to her lip when she pictures the wobble
of his waltz. She walks to the pot and feels
its sides, cool enough to cradle. She takes
handfuls and pats out rows of even cakes.

V. Anna at the Ironing Board, Dec. 7-1913

She wraps a towel around her hand and takes
the iron from the stove. She was soaking Abe's shirts
last night—in blue-bag mixed with hartshorn flakes
to fend moths—when she heard his snoring first
grow shallow and weak. Collars: now wan
as snow on unbroken ground. Fifteen years
she scrubbed mud from oilskin and spent denim,
while beyond the Forty Mile, his scattered
tailing-piles grew round as burial mounds.
She holds the iron close to her cheek, feeling
its glow a moment, then takes his shirt down
from the drying-rack. She rubs on sealing
wax to hold each crease. Two men swinging spades
sift for gold in black sand turned from Abe's grave.

JOAN RAWLINS BIGGAR • MARYSVILLE, WASHINGTON

Untangling A Wilderness

The Abercrombie Trail, All-American Route to the Gold Fields

C hilkoot Pass—Dawson—the Klondike. Magic words in 1898, conjuring images of gold for the taking. Two hundred thousand people from all walks of life, many terrifyingly incompetent to survive the rigors of the northland, borrowed, mortgaged, or sold all they possessed and stampeded toward the gold fields.

Most American prospectors sailed from West Coast cities, mainly Seattle, to the Lynn Canal in Southeast Alaska. They disembarked at Skagway or nearby Dyea, then struggled over the coastal mountains via Skagway's White Pass or Dyea's Chilkoot Pass. Once over the passes, Canadian officials met them at the border to collect duty on their supplies. Only then could they tackle the four hundred miles of Canadian wilderness which lay between them and their hoped for Eldorados.

The prospectors clamored for an all-American route which would avoid the onerous duties. The U.S. government, uneasy about protecting its own interests in the north, ordered the army to commission exploring expeditions to look for such a route and to find out more about its vast northern territory.

Enter William Ralph Abercrombie, an early-day Indiana Jones who deserves to be better known by those of us who benefited from his efforts to untangle the Alaskan wilderness.

During the earlier Russian occupation of Alaska, an Indian fur-trading route ran from the Copper River over the mountains to the head of Valdez Arm on Prince William Sound. The Copper River Indians had abandoned their trail following a fearful smallpox epidemic among the natives on Prince William Sound. Some guidebooks, mixing rumor and imagination with the meager known facts, picked up on stories about the lost trail. They suggested Valdez as an easier, all-American entrance to fortune.

Klondike Gold Rush Centennial Anthology

At least six thousand stampeders did cross the Valdez Glacier, heading for the Copper River country where "nuggets as big as birds' eggs" supposedly lay scattered on the river banks. These hopefuls faced all the hardships confronted by the prospectors going to the Klondike, but few found a golden reward. For most, destitution, starvation, sickness, or death waited along their trail.

The toll for these unfortunates would have been far worse but for the help of the U.S. Army and Captain William Ralph Abercrombie.

Abercrombie Returns to Alaska

Back in the summer of 1884, Second Lieutenant Abercrombie was a twenty-seven year old career army officer. Intelligent and articulate, the big, sandy-haired young man had fought Indians and kept the peace in mining camps across the American west. Then he was sent to command a difficult exploring expedition from tidewater in southern Prince William Sound up the Copper River. He was searching for an all-American route into Alaska's interior. But shallow, shifting delta channels, glaciers discharging icebergs into the river, whirlpools and rapids, all made the upriver passage impossibly dangerous.

However, during that expedition, natives told him about the lost Valdez trail. He'd taken a side trip to climb the Valdez Glacier. His guides pointed out the direction from which the early Indian fur traders had come, but he didn't believe they'd used the glacier route.

In 1898, now a captain, the burly officer again found himself at Valdez, in command of one of the three exploring expeditions the U.S. Army had commissioned. He was to look for an all-American route to the gold fields, to find out all he could about the land and its native inhabitants, and to help protect American interests in the north.

Abercrombie and his men left Seattle for Valdez on April 7, 1898, aboard the ship Valencia. Also aboard were gold seekers and the members of another expedition which intended to land in Cook Inlet (where modern

Anchorage would someday grow).

The army had arranged for shipment of more than 500 reindeer from Norway to Haines, on Alaska's Lynn Canal. With the reindeer were Lapland herders to care for them. These animals were supposed to transport supplies for the explorers, as well as provide food for starving and stranded gold seekers. But the long sea journey had left the deer too weak for either purpose, so the ship steamed on to Dyea. Abercrombie tried to get pack mules from Army personnel stationed there, without success. Frustrated, he asked that horses be sent on the Valencia's next trip north.

Landing at Valdez

They sailed back down the Lynn Canal and up the coast to Prince William Sound, where fourteen years earlier Abercrombie had made his first attempt to reach the Copper River Valley.

Snow lay seven feet deep on the shore when on April 18, explorers and prospectors landed at Valdez Inlet near the present town of Valdez and the site of today's Alyeska oil pipeline terminal. Over six hundred tons of supplies for Abercrombie and the prospectors lay jumbled together in the hold of the ship.

After sorting the boxes and bags into smaller boats, the men beached the vessels at low water mark. Soldiers and prospectors spent a trying day packing awkward bundles three hundred yards across the ice-covered mud flats. The heavy loads badly bruised the mens' shoulders and backs. Their clothing became soaked. That night, exhausted, they spread their blankets to sleep on the snow. Though the thermometer reached eight degrees below zero, Captain Abercrombie reported, "Not a grumble was heard from any of the party."

Off to Explore

Besides Captain Abercrombie, the expedition included First Lieutenant Guy H. Preston, Lieutenant Lowe, Lieutenant Brookfield, three men from the Hospital Corps, two guides, a geologist, and fifteen enlisted men. Many of their names now title geographical features on the map of Alaska, but at the time their purpose was to chart territory largely unknown by non-natives.

After establishing their camp and a depot at Valdez Inlet, the men split up to try to reach and explore the valley of the Copper River.

On April 22, Abercrombie sent the topographical officer, Lieutenant Lowe, and guide Harvey Robe, to follow a tumultuous stream, which he named the Lowe, into and through the Keystone Canyon. Then, as today, waterfalls plunged over vertical canyon walls, which in places pressed so close together the river nearly had to turn on its side to get through. Tangled brush and trees choked the way. As Abercrombie had suspected, this narrow break in the mountain wall proved to be not only the passage once used by the Copper River Indian traders, but also the key to the longed for route to the gold fields.

Meanwhile, Lieutenant Guy Preston's party made the difficult crossing into Alaska's interior via the Valdez Glacier, which at the time descended to within five miles of tidewater.

On May 4, after a week-long blizzard on the glacier, Abercrombie left camp with additional supplies for the Preston party. He and his men wrestled hand sleds, each loaded with up to one hundred fifty pounds, over a series of steep, icy benches to reach the nearly five thousand foot summit. On the glacier, they found about seven hundred prospectors also struggling toward the interior.

One of these prospectors, Luther Guitteau, with his three partners, had supplies totaling more than three tons. "...every individual pound of that six thousand pound total," he wrote later, " was a heartbreaking load at some stages of that ascent."

Many hopefuls gave up the grueling work before they reached the summit. Abercrombie noted that the average age of the prospectors he met was about forty-seven, and that many of them had failed in numerous business ventures. On one of the benches, Guitteau said, "two men died in one night from exhaustion, overwork, and poor food. Friends...buried them under seven feet of snow in a little draw."

Some of the prospectors used horses, burros, even dogs, to help with their freight. Others rigged line and pulley systems to help hoist the sleds over the steep places. The government men found many prospectors better equipped than they. Abercrombie decided they'd never successfully explore the country without pack animals.

Pack Horses to the Rescue

The Valencia returned from the south on May 24. The requested horses were not aboard. An exasperated Captain Abercrombie sailed to Seattle, then crossed the Cascade mountains to the Yakima Indian Reservation where he personally purchased forty head of stock.

Upon his return to Valdez, Abercrombie directed Lieutenant Lowe to select some of the toughest of the pack animals. He asked Lowe to cross the softening snow of the Valdez Glacier and then proceed to the Yukon.

Meanwhile, Abercrombie organized the remaining men into four groups to explore as much of the region as possible. Part of the expedition was to follow Lowe over Valdez Glacier.

A Change In Plans

When Lowe sent back word that he did not "consider the glacier feasible for animals from now until snow packs," Abercrombie changed his plan. He decided to take all four expedition sections with him up the Lowe River and into the interior via Keystone Canyon.

With a packer and two horses, he set out on July 18 to prospect trail to the canyon. They crossed a number of wild, rain-swollen glacial streams. Prospectors camping by one particularly ugly torrent advised Abercrombie that they'd tried and failed to get across.

Abercrombie prided himself on never sending his men where he would not go himself. And, wrote the Captain, since "...it was absolutely necessary to cross this [river] if I went in via Lowe River, I disregarded all advice...and rode

Klondike Gold Rush Centennial Anthology 9

my horse into the stream...believing that if my horse could carry my weight (215 pounds) the pack animals that I intended to load with but 150 pounds could also cross. When in midstream, I heard the bowlders [sic] being washed down the river bottom, and knew that I was in serious trouble.

"I pushed on some five or 10 yards with the water up to my horse's shoulder when the animal was struck by one of those bowlders, carried off his feet, and washed some 150 yards downstream, rolling over and over in the torrent, while I clung to his mane with my right hand...

"At about the same time the horse lodged against a large rock with his feet uppermost, with my body pinned under him. I let go of the mane and grabbed the animal by the tail...the horse scrambled up the bank and pulled me up with him."

To bridge the swollen stream and cut trail through the canyon would take the rest of the working season. Abercrombie had been nearly paralyzed by the frigid water. His hand, struck by his horse's hoof, had swelled to twice normal size. The bruised and battered captain decided to attempt the glacier crossing despite Lieutenant Lowe's misgivings.

Crossing the Glacier

One of the enlisted men, Private Bence, proved adept at laying out trail over the glacier. For several days he marked the safest passage around crevasses and over the weakening snow bridges while others moved their camp to the glacier and shoed the Indian ponies.

By July 27 the expedition was ready to go, but nothing seemed to come easily for the explorers. Fog moved in, followed by rain. Bacon and ham turned into masses of mold in the high humidity. Sugar dissolved into syrup.

While waiting for the weather to improve, the expedition rescued eight prospectors who had been lost on the glacier for five days. Raving of glacier demons, in their panic they'd abandoned even their food and extra clothing.

Despite continuing rain and fog, on August 5 Abercrombie decided they could wait no longer. Private Bence led the way up the glacier from monument to monument. The captain followed with his horse, on which he'd packed a five-gallon keg of whiskey. The expedition proceeded in sections of five horses, each led by a man, each section with an extra man and rope.

The horses sensed danger. Trembling, they pressed their noses against the backs of the men leading them. When they broke through the rotting snow bridging the crevasses, they lay perfectly still until the men pulled them out. In places the trail was so steep and narrow that now and then a horse would slip and tumble to the bottom. Though often leaving behind a trail of blood, the plucky horses kept going.

Men and beasts struggled upward until the night became too black to go any further. The men tethered the pack animals to ice hummocks, scattered the horse's grain on the ice, and removed their loads. They left the saddles and blankets on to give some protection from the icy rain.

The men suffered along with the horses. They gulped their canned meat, cheese, and hard tack, and no one refused his tin cupful of Abercrombie's whiskey. They spent the rest of the night tramping back and forth behind the picket line.

In a report gripping as any adventure novel, Abercrombie wrote, "During my twenty-two years of service on the frontier I never experienced a more desolate and miserable night. ...Occasionally the mighty glacier would crack...with a vibration that would cause the men to stop in their tramp and the horses to nicker with...fear. Then would follow a deafening roar as some thousands of tons of ice were detached from one of the hundreds of glaciers that fringed the mountain sides."

Echoes thundered about them, then died away down the valley thousands of feet below.

The next day a hurricane blew through the pass into the interior. Gusts of rain and snow froze as fast as they struck, coating men and horses with armor of ice. Landmarks, even other expedition members, were invisible

Klondike Gold Rush Centennial Anthology

in the storm.

If they turned to the right or left the sleet cut their faces. Fortunately, the wind at their backs kept them from straying onto the great icefields surrounding the pass and after hours of struggle, they reached the summit in its exact center.

The men rounded a high cliff. "Behind the shelter of this rocky cliff there was a perfect haven of rest and sunshine," Abercrombie wrote, "while out of the pass rushed the howling storm like the water out of the nozzle of a fire hose."

Men and pack animals reveled in the sunshine while it melted away their icy armor. They had crossed the Valdez Glacier at a season of the year when no one thought it possible, in twenty-nine consecutive hours without sleep, rest, or shelter. Soon they were ready to press on with their explorations.

Exploring the Copper River Country

Several days later, the civilians and Corporal Heiden's section went back to Valdez. Heiden was to begin work on Abercrombie's trail through Keystone Canyon while the other sections explored the Copper River country.

As the explorers worked their way toward the Copper River, they passed many prospectors, all complaining because they lacked transportation and decent trails. Because they could not carry enough food, many had sold their outfits and turned back.

Game in the area had vanished with the onslaught of gold seekers. As the result of their carelessness with campfires in the dry interior, entire valleys were afire. Abercrombie's men and horses had to dodge burning, falling trees.

The expedition finally arrived at the new miners' settlement of Copper Center and divided again.

Abercrombie's section pushed on into the interior, as far as the east branch of the Tok River. There Indians pointed out a pass which they said led to the gold fields. By then their supplies were dangerously low. Floating their gear downriver by raft so that the horses could move faster through the timber, he and his packers started back the one hundred seventy-five miles to Copper Center.

At the settlement, they heard that sections two and three had been wrecked while crossing a river. They'd lost one man and all their food. Abercrombie collected provisions and boated down the Copper River to rescue the hungry men.

Following the Copper as it cut through the mountains on its way to the sea, they stopped to reconnoiter at the head of what is now Abercrombie Rapids, just above Miles Glacier. This three-mile stretch of wild water squeezed between a high rock wall on one side and glacial moraine on the other. Fourteen years earlier, on Abercrombie's first expedition to Alaska, the rapids had blocked his upriver passage to the interior.

Below the rapids, the Miles and Childs glaciers faced each other across the Copper. They had shrunk greatly since Abercrombie's first visit, and the river's channels were much wider. The current, though less violent, was still unnavigable for upriver travel. The party shot the rapids and reached the Copper River Delta without mishap. On October 16, 1898, the weary men arrived at Valdez. They'd traveled more than eight hundred miles by foot, horseback, raft, and boat since August 5, and winter was at hand.

Before he'd left Valdez, Abercrombie had contacted authorities, urging that the expedition be continued the following season.

He had asked a trusted employee, Quartermaster's Agent Charles Brown, to open the reply to his report. If authorities gave the go ahead, Brown should build stables and storehouses for winter use. Upon his return, Abercrombie found the buildings finished, constructed by returning miners in payment for aid the army gave them.

Within a few days all sections completed their parts of the work. At last, Americans had a viable route of their own to the gold fields, although most of Abercrombie's trail remained to be built.

Klondike Gold Rush Centennial Anthology 13

The Winter of '98 - '99

By October of '98, 75 per cent of the discontented and "green" prospectors had left the Copper River country.

Abercrombie sailed south to collect supplies and to plan for the next season's construction. Charles Brown, left in charge at Valdez, made a revealing comment in view of the disaster to come that winter: "The army ration has proved insufficient for the necessities of the men here...Fish, in the greatest abundance, and huckleberries and salmon berries...have given a most desirable change."

The army rations and those of the gold seekers were about the same: bacon, flour, hard tack, sugar, beans, rice. When winter came and the remaining prospectors had to survive on the food they'd carried into the interior, a terrible and little understood scourge struck—scurvy.

Disaster

Luther Guitteau, among the miners waiting out the winter at Copper Center, told of the doctor who'd dropped in to say he was treating two men in the next cabin for rheumatism or scurvy, he didn't know which.

"Very soon we were to know," said Guitteau, "with awful accuracy, the symptoms and effects of the disease [scurvy] which turned men's blood to water, brought on lassitude and weakness, and finally left them to die of starvation..."

Few miners knew that green foods and fresh meat would stave off the disease. "My own preventative measures," Guitteau shared with those willing to listen, "consisted mainly of eating fresh moose meat...and raw evaporated onions soaked in vinegar."

Mr. Guitteau helped care for the very ill who were brought in daily from isolated camps. Those still well and the sick who could still get around set out to make the midwinter crossing over the Glacier to Valdez.

By February the only able-bodied men in Copper Center were the handful on the hospital staff. They could only pray that those who reached Valdez had alerted the government men to their situation.

Finally, late in April, Guitteau "heard the grand news that Captain Abercrombie had returned to Valdez..."

He was not the only one relieved at Abercrombie's return. Quartermaster's Agent Charles Brown exclaimed, "...Captain, it has been clear hell! I tell you the early days of Montana were not a marker to what I have gone through this winter!" He'd cared for approximately one hundred sick, destitute prospectors, some of whom rested in the new graveyard.

Abercrombie organized a relief center in Valdez, then sent drivers and dog teams over the glacier to bring out the sick men. Only then could he start turning the Abercrombie Trail into the Trans-Alaskan Military Wagon Road.

The Road

Abercrombie put many of the destitute prospectors to work on the road, or other government projects around Valdez.

Prospector Luther Guitteau found no gold, but "something in the Interior country" got into his blood. He decided to stay. He went to work for Captain Abercrombie as cook for the bridge and trail gang who cleared the timber and bridged the glacial streams that tumbled down the sides of Keystone Canyon.

The brush and timber were cleared and rivers bridged by use of hand tools only. By October 10, 1899, a road suitable for pack horses extended from Valdez ninety-three miles into the interior.

Within the next few years, the road reached several hundred miles to Eagle, with a branch to Fairbanks. Wagons used it in the summer, horse-drawn sleds in winter. The first automobile drove from Valdez to Fairbanks in 1913. Today thousands of travelers roll along the Richardson Highway, Abercrombie's all-American route to the interior.

William Ralph Abercrombie played an exciting, important part in the development of America's Last Frontier. Though not as well known as Indiana Jones or some other explorers, Abercrombie himself knew the value of his contributions.

Years later he said, "It is seldom given a man to witness the results of the developing of a country that he has explored, and I take not a little satisfaction in looking back...to my struggle to untangle a small part of this wilderness."

The End

JAMES GURLEY • SEATTLE, WASHINGTON

Views Of The Klondike Route

-A.E. Hegg exhibits his Gold Rush photographs
in New York City, 1898-

I won't go into all they endure:
the sourdoughs in my photographs
who claim any hill promises profit,
who thaw the ground in winter,
digging, so that come spring
gold nuggets wash through the sluices,
their hands cracked and raw
from pickax and shovel.

Only to go back to the saloon in Dawson,
supplies gone, the card game rigged,
nowhere to sleep but the dirt floor.
They make tall tales of their misery:
a makeshift boat that nearly capsizes
in unpredictable Lake Bennett,
muskeg, mosquitoes along the mire-
marked road to this Eldorado.

No heroics or easy plunder in my pictures.
Instead, a man cooking on his Yukon stove,
a pack mule train in Box Canyon,
the banks of the Yukon River a ragged
scallop of boats and scows,
or the Stampeder I caught unawares,
sleeping beside the trail from Dyea.

At the exhibit they crowd around each photograph.
Even the one of my first darkroom.
That light-leaking affair fastened to my sledge,
held secure by luck and rope. Dragged up
Chilkoot Pass, that human trail I photographed
with my bulky camera in a blizzard,
the climbers dark specks in deep furrows of snow.
Lunacy. Developing these pictures
in the slushy chemical bath
while freezing rain shakes the canvas walls.

Later, in Dawson, I built
a studio from whipsawed logs.
Painted *Views of the Klondike Route*
on the side. These words advertising
life in the tier of mines on Cheechako Hill,
miners waiting their turn to register claims,
Skookum Jim posing with his pickax,
Little Ruby singing at the Monte Carlo.

I don't dream of gold.
But of being there when someone
strikes it rich, or gives up his lease.
Works for wages, for fare home.
Try explaining that to these New York gawkers
who've never seen streams of yellow dust
more plentiful than food, the sun
at midnight, or fields littered with dead horses,
creek beds criss-crossed with sluice-boxes.

It takes cops to quell this mini-stampede,
as if each photograph records their adventure
north and back, victorious, a millionaire;
as if they, too, longed for this crazy scheme
beyond a sweatshop or dull office work,
enough to fuel a hope, almost a riot
in the streets, people shoving for just a glimpse
of glittering bars stacked taller than a man,
astonished it's more than fool's gold.

Sister Skagway

My name is Sister Damian Aloysius Geoffrey, order of the Servants of Our Lady. I know of no other way to begin the story of my violent act except with my name. In the end, of course, you may judge. I have judged; Almighty God has judged. The good, if often misguided, people of Skagway, Alaska Territory, have judged me. I will not mislead you at any turn of the trail: they have found me guilty.

I have appealed my sentence to the territorial magistrate up in Dyea and have been told that he will telegraph the appeal directly, if necessary, to President McKinley and will intervene in person in Skagway if he receives a proper answer. If it please the Lord, I will meet him prior to tomorrow morning. If such intervention does not please the Lord, I fear that I will be escorted to the gallows to meet the Lord in person. My escort on such a fateful trip will be, of course, Mister Lanny Pinchot, first crony to that notorious lawless scoundrel, Mister Jefferson R. Smith. For days, now, I have listened to Mister Pinchot's footfall on the heavy plank stairs. Nine clumps up to my storage cell above Clancy's Saloon. Nine down. Four times daily. His rhythmic steps are as regular as the cadence in Gregorian Chant.

As this may well be my last night, I intend to set down my entire story notwithstanding the smoke from pipes and cigars that escapes from the saloon below and wafts up through my floorboards to the yellowed ceiling above. I look up and see tattered newspapers from as far back as 1897 and up to early 1898, tacked up as insulation. My seat is a wooden crate that had been used to transport wolf traps to this city. The cell is exactly five and one-half paces wide by three paces deep.

The shelves had been emptied long before my arrival—the storage room being the favored hoosegow of Mister Jefferson R. Smith's band of rowdies. Its tiny window is reinforced with seven iron beams. No matter; it is far too high for me to use even if I stand on the crate.

Into the plank door, a hatch half the size of the window
has been cut. It can be opened from the outside only. I am
constantly being taunted and watched. Without comment,
I will say—and then speak no more of the subject—that I
have not a whit of privacy. I am fed twice daily and then,
an hour later, am led barefoot, from the cell to the bawdy
house adjacent to the saloon to utilize its facilities.
Apparently, my jailers feel I am a threat to escape, to verily knock down the storehouse door. I have assured them
that I have no intention of making an escape...although if
the opportunity presented itself wherein I might proceed
from these confines to others and be on with the Lord's
mission, I should surely take it, in daylight or darkness.
There is little home of such. My shredded habit would give
me away, my filthy wimple serving as a beacon.

Already, the slops and swill of demon rum has begun
to turn the men into debauchers. They have cast aside
their wives and mothers and children and come in search
of gold, an honest man's honest dream. After all, God's
house is adorned with gold. Their folly, of course, lies in
the devil's own brew found in the saloons and sins of the
flesh from the dance halls. The men sink to discourse in
profanity. They imbibe to excess and fornicate freely, trading their pokes for a momentary stifling of the
concupiscent urge. By comparison, Judas was an
archangel!

Eighteen months ago, I had been assigned to bring
the Word of the Lord to the miners in DawsonCity, Yukon
Territory. I was chosen for the arduous task because of my
upbringing in the Cascade Mountains east of Seattle. I am
a most able woman of stout pioneer stock, being quite
competent with rifle, rope and pack animal.

I arrived in sinful Skagway, the gateway to the
Klondike gold fields, to find a renegade town of 4,000
souls run by a band of dishonest grifters, pickpockets,
bunco experts and ruffians. When the Lord wrote the ten
commandments, he must have been visualizing Skagway,
Alaska Territory.

By May of 1898, dozens of ramshackle buildings had
sprung up. Ten thousand more men had arrived...as did

more card cheats, unsavory ladies and outright assassins. But I have leaped ahead of myself.

As I had been assigned to Dawson City, I secured passage over the treacherous 32-mile Chilkoot Trail as a member of a caravan of merchants. At Finnegan's Point, I chanced to slip on a loose bit of shale. Verily, my Achilles tendon was sliced and my ankle shattered. So severe was my injury that my leg was spliced to my rifle—a fine 30/40 Krag carbine that was given as a present from my prior parish—and I was littered back to Dyea, and thence further back to Skagway for recuperation. Oh, I have fully recovered in the ensuing 18 months but I fear I shall always drag my left leg slightly off kilter from the right. Lord knows, it's nothing that I cannot endure and I daily offer up this inconvenience for the poor souls in purgatory. The lasting shame of the incident was my loss of two volumes of world history and my collection of Henry James. My superiors, when notified of my predicament, ordered my to do what I could for the burgeoning townspeople of this gateway town. Unfortunately, Skagway—thanks primarily to Mister Jefferson R. Smith—heeds neither the word of law nor the Word of God. But I have stayed these months, ever countenancing the orders of my superiors and witnessing the madness brought on by whiskey and isolation.

Now I can hear the rhythmic clunk of boots up the back stairs. It belongs to Mister Lanny Pinchot, a squint-eyed scoundrel of the first order. He will be bringing my evening meal for which I am fairly well famished. Quite a fine meal, I should add, as it is the same food fed to the bawdy house ladies. For such, I say a silent prayer of thanks for my captors for feeding me as well as they do their harlots. They also allow me the use of the bawdy house *salle de bain* twice daily as well. Barefoot, as I have mentioned.

"Sister. Sister! You awake in there?" Mister Pinchot rattles the wooden door. "Stand back." Then he opens the hatch. I see his scabby, unshaven face leering in at me. He has a mouth filled of perfectly white teeth, except for a single black hole where an incisor once was.

Klondike Gold Rush Centennial Anthology

"Did you expect that I'd escaped your fortress, Mister Lanny Pinchot?"

"No, ma'am. It's held meaner galoots than you. "
When not speaking, Mister Pinchot has a nasty habit of filling the gap between his teeth with the pink tip of his tongue. Quite distasteful.

"You brought my dinner, I expect?"

"Yes, ma'am. Stay against the far wall."

I could hear him lift the closure beam from the door. He set the meal on the floor and quickly closed the door, almost as if he expected me to leap at him. As hungry as I was, I wanted more to know if any word had been received from the magistrate in Dyea. But I dared not ask this charlatan. I would make contact with my confidante at the bawdy house later in the evening. All I said was, "I expect you'll be back in an hour to escort me downstairs?"

"Yes, ma'am. Soapy wants you to have all the comforts of home. He was real sharp on what he told me: feed and fertilize her twicet a day."

"Mister Pinchot! "

"Sorry, Sister."

"Can you tell me any news of the town?"

"Judge Van Horn's been drunk as a hoot since he found you guilty..."

"...and well he should be. "

"He's the law, ma'am. And you never denied shooting crazy Two Chew."

"And I never shall." Imagine! Did he expect me to lie? "Mister Two Chew Calderone was violating that young woman..."

"Look, Sister, that young woman was a dollar-a-dance slut. Whole town knew it. Now you ain't a bad sort and I'm sorry they're going to string you up but you killed a friend a mine so I ain't too sorry. "

The vision of Two Chew Calderone leaped in front of me. Suddenly, I wanted neither to eat nor to continue the discussion with Mister Pinchot. Apparently he didn't either because the door slammed shut and I heard his boots thud along the planking and down the stairs.

My violent act involving the late Mister Two Chew

Calderone began as a result of children. One of my ministries is to provide for the orphans of Skagway. If you can imagine, this city of less than two years has produced four orphans. Far be it from me to be able to sustain without help four infants while maintaining my spiritual practice. Thank the Lord, who always has a way of providing, that two of the infants' mothers have seen fit to leave the bawdy houses and come live with me and the children. However, God has chosen me to be the mainstay for them all. The few Christian folk in town come to our aid but the mantle of provider falls on these shoulders.

As it was early in the fall, the moose weren't close to town yet but I had to bring one home before the snows made hunting most impossible. I needed a season's fare for the children. It's enough to know that I'd gone out almost five miles to the Devil's Punchbowl and seen barely a track. On my return, as I neared town, I spotted a fine, majestic bull munching alder bark on the city side of Lower Dewey Lake. He was not more than 75 yards away! If I could get him, I could at the very least field-dress him and return for the meat on the morrow, hopefully with help.

I unslung the Krag and chambered one of its five rounds. Softly, almost as in prayer, I gathered my skirts and knelt on one knee. I brought the valley of the rifle's rear sight to the bull and then pushed back my wimple. I snugged the buttplate to my shoulder and then set the forward sight on the bull's neck. He lifted his head but did not seem to notice me. Silently, I mouthed, "My Mother, My Confidence," barely touching the trigger. The bull's forelegs collapsed but he rose almost as fast as he'd gone down. Quickly, I chambered a second round and fired. This shot broke his neck.

Night had fallen by the time I'd quartered him. It took all my strength to winch the quarters up over lodgepole-pine branches. Each quarter hung like a white ghost in the dark Arctic night. At least my moose would not become wolf food. Leaving my gear cached under the same pine, I loaded the moose's nourishing liver into my rucksack and lit out for town. I quite literally had to drag myself along

Klondike Gold Rush Centennial Anthology 23

the trail. My game leg pulsed in pain. At the town's edge, more precisely at Captain Moore's Wharf, I heard a woman's scream. I slipped from my rucksack and half slid, half stumbled down the embankment only to find Mister Two Chew Calderone, by light of an oil torch, stomping on the arm of Miss Melissa Bonteller, one of the ladies who had eschewed life in a bawdy house.

I ran toward them, screaming as loudly as Miss Bonteller. Mister Calderone, his britches at his knees but his long johns covering his indecency, quite backhanded me a blow so solid I reeled back and did not know that I'd been struck until I was face down on the bank. I rolled to my back and shouted, "Stop! Stop! Help!" Mister Calderone cuffed Miss Bonteller across the face and approached me. I cannot repeat his words. It is enough to say his vulgar stream of invective would have garnered him more than a rosary in the confessional. He began kicking me until I rolled down the bank to the water's edge. He hobbled down and put his boot on my neck, crushing my face into the gravel. When he seemed satisfied that I would no longer interrupt his horror, he returned to Miss Bonteller and knelt over her.

I spied my deadly Krag and crawled to it. When I had it pointed at him, I shouted, "Stop! For the love of God, stop! Please!"

Mister Calderone turned. Much to my absolute amazement, he snorted. Viscous mucus sprayed from his nostrils. He twisted his mouth into a pucker and...spit at me. And laughed!

"Get off her," I ordered.

"Hah! You going to plug me, Sister Skagway?" He stood up and, quite mockingly, put his hands over his head. "Go ahead. Shoot."

"I know you. "

He said, "You don't know anything. What could a nun know?"

I ignored the personal degradation. "Leave the girl be," I demanded.

"The girl is almost as old as you, Sister Skagway." He started toward me. I clearly heard the gravel crunch under his boots. The light from the oil torch made his beard seem to glow. I admit to not being sure what to do. Because I had been brought up the daughter of a mountain rancher and quite comfortable around firearms, I never endured a moment's fear when facing a hunting target. Now, however, a man, a vile devil of a man, approached. Miss Bonteller writhed behind him, holding her stomach.

"Come no further," I said.

"Oh, I'll come further," he said, not ten paces from me. "I'll come further and I'll take that rifle for my own and then I'll take you before I finish with the slut. You don't understand that I'm a deputy marshal!. Made so by Soapy Smith himself."

" Stop... please. "I was begging him but I admit, I chambered a round. "Miss Bonteller is not a... what you said. Not any more. Please leave us be."

"You meddling hag. I'll have to show you something you haven't ever seen."

Five paces away, he said, "You're not supposed to point a gun at anything you didn't intend to shoot?" Three paces.

When I fired, I did not hear the explosion. I believe to this day, some two weeks after the act, I saw the bullet enter his chest and exit from his back tumbling end-over-end. He didn't move, didn't fall. He looked down at the hole in his perky and watched it dampen. He looked at me, his eyes evil, taunting, sinfully gleeful. Then astonished, as if he just been given the secret to a most complex puzzle. "Sister," he said, and fell onto the embankment, his head crashing face first into the gravel.

Because he was one of Mister Jefferson Smith's henchmen, I was tried by Mister Smith's judge. And here I sit. On a wooden crate that brought wolf traps to Skagway, my dinner cold and Mister Two Chew Calderone long since given a hero's burial, a flag draped over his spruce casket. And I still see that round from the Krag tumbling out of Mister Two Chew Calderone. It tumbled and tumbled to... I don't know where. There must have been an alternative solution to my predicament. If I really had to shoot, I could have shot him in the leg. Perhaps, I could have held him at bay while Miss Bonteller escaped. Then I could have run to town. I might have fired one round or two as warnings to him... and still have a last round in case the warnings failed. So many better choices than the one I had made.

The methodical footfall on the planks returns me to cognizance. My dinner remains on the plank floor. It is quite cold but my respite had filled me with ravishment. I would not have time to eat before being led to the bawdy house. Hopefully, Mister Lanny Pinchot will see the kindness in allowing me to eat after my visit below.

"You awake in there?" The door rattled and the hatch opened.

I lifted my chin slightly, showing him in no uncertain terms that I am in full control of my faculties and that no amount of incarceration will weaken me. "Yes. "

"Ready to go?"

"Quite. "

I see his tongue fill the gap between his teeth. Then he says, "Off with the boots."

"Really, Mister Pinchot, don't you think..."

"Soapy says you go barefoot when you go out and that's that."

"God have mercy on him. And you." I take to my lantern crate and unfasten my boot laces.

The nine plank steps are rough on my feet. I fear for splinters, barely notice the fall chill. Inside the bawdy house, I am greeted as warmly as if I were a consort. The young ladies, remarkably the ones who scorned me over the past two years—quite understandably so because I did nothing to endear myself to them—have taken my plight to heart. In the past three days, they have developed a pattern. They are at once sympathetic and helpful; warm and caring. Whereas once they were my enemies—and I still wholeheartedly disagree with their chosen life—they are now cordial. They, each and to a person, have come to me to express their appreciation for what they call a valiant act. They have even taken in the two fallen-away ladies-of-the-night and the four babies from my home. It is preciously evil of them to mock Mister Jefferson R. Smith but they do. He had ordered them to evict the turncoats and the children after my conviction. But the ladies spoke in a single voice to him, swearing to him that they would forever stop plying their trade if he did not allow this bit of Christian charity into the bawdy house. They told me of Mr. Smith's extreme displeasure and, hastened to add, that it may have precipitated the unusual rapidity of my future hanging. However, we all laughingly agreed it was, somehow, a raw brand of northern justice that he should be so perturbed. I, understandably, laughed somewhat less than the others but nonetheless, enjoyed the spirit of the humor.

Now that I am inside the bawdy house, the ladies shoo Mister Pinchot to the bar, one lady using all her wiles to distract his attention. They explain that this is accomplished with relative ease but I avert my eyes at the subject. Then, they tend my feet, giving me plush beaver slippers to wear. I marvel at the grand spectacle of the greeting room. Its wall are of red velvet. Golden lamps cast soft, dewey shadows over the couches. The ladies all wave; their gentlemen callers hide their faces. As well they should.

Then, one of the young ladies shows me to a private room with a wash basin. One always stands guard to insure my privacy. Tonight, it was Miss Melissa Bonteller, my confidante. We embraced and she inquired as to my well being…she, who had been brutally beaten by Mister Two Chew Calderone. It was she who I had asked to take my appeal to the magistrate in Dyea. When I inquired as to a response, she downcasts her eyes. Knowing that I am to meet the gallows at morning sun-up unless interrupted by a reprieve, we both realize the depth of her gesture.

A cloud begins to grow in my stomach. Tears well in her eyes, one still puffy from the thrashing. "They'll be no tears on my account, young lady," I said.

"Are you afraid, Sister?"

"Of death? Not at all. It's the natural way of things. I would fear my eternal damnation for my violent act if I were certain that I had done wrong. Alas! I suppose I am doomed to vacillate about my guilt until the trap door springs open beneath my feet. I know now that I could have done otherwise. At the time of the act, I did not. "

She embraced me as if I were a long lost sister. Then I said, "The Lord is just; the Lord is merciful. Pray for the latter so we may meet again. "

A rap sounds on the door. Mister Pinchot. "Okey dokey, Sister. Time's up. "

At least this time Mister Lanny Pinchot cannot look in on me. I whisper to Miss Bonteller, "You'll be sure to get word to me if you hear anything from the magistrate?"

"He said he'd come personally if there was a satisfactory answer to his telegram. "

Poor Miss Bonteller looked almost sadder than she did that night on the beach. I took her tiny chin in my hand. "Be strong, sister. The Lord will provide." Then I touched her cheek with my lips, adjusted my wimple and strode to the door to meet Mister Pinchot. Back in my cell, I ate my cold dinner and began the Sorrowful Mysteries of the rosary.

Now, I hear a bootfall on the first step. The sun is barely lighting the sky. Step two. Step three. It is as if each bootfall is grinding another part of me into the beach gravel under Captain Moore's Wharf. Step five. Step six. Then the footfalls stop...

JANE GUILBAULT • ROCHESTER, NEW YORK

Discovery

Almost as if they heard you whisper
that word, they come cartwheeling
into town to pan overland,
spurred into snowfall.

Sacks full, they fill their stomachs
with smallmouth bass and return
always to cradles, to rock
sand and water, sifting asleep.

Black smoke curls up over
the hills signaling we are no longer
alone under the shade of sky.
What did we know would unravel

that summer you splashed
your copper legs in the creek
and washed out our coffee cups
only to find gold in the gravel?

JOHN W. WASHBURN • NORTHVILLE, NEW YORK

The Mayor Of Dawson City

How did a poor Adirondack farm boy become a multi-millionaire, and own the richest city in North America?

(June 15, 1897 - San Francisco) The Steamship *Excelsior* arrived early in the morning from St. Michaels, Alaska. Aboard were forty very rich men from the Klondike region of the Yukon Valley in Canada. Foremost among these was Joseph Ladue, who some reporters referred to as the Mayor of Dawson City. He might more accurately have been called the owner of Dawson City, for he did indeed own a major portion of it. The parts that he did not own were the parts he had already sold.

Also aboard was over two million dollars in gold dust and nuggets that these men had dug out of the frozen ground. The exception was Joe Ladue. While everyone else had staked and claimed goldmines, he had staked and claimed a townsite. Ladue had only brought out $170,000 in gold, but his holdings in the Klondike were worth over $5,000,000.

With the arrival of the steamship *Portland* in Seattle two days later, carrying over two tons of gold, the greatest gold rush stampede the world had every seen, before or since, was set in motion. Without the foresight and influence of Joseph Ladue, it is unlikely that this great gold strike would have happened as it did. Without the gold rush, the deep economic depression that gripped the country and the world since 1893, may have continued for years to come.

Who was Joe Ladue? Where had he come from? How did he happen to be in just the right place at just the right time? Was he a genius, or was he just plain lucky?

Joe was born in Schuyler Falls, a small Clinton County community in the northern Adirondack Mountains of New York State. He was the second of five children. His father was Francis Ladue, a French-Canadian bricklayer and his mother's name was Mary Pelky Ladue. Few details are known of Joe's early childhood, except that he was a very quick learner and did fairly well in school. He was a seri-

Klondike Gold Rush Centennial Anthology 31

ous fox hunter and an accomplished trapper of muskrat.

Joseph's mother died in 1861 when he was seven years old. He and his older sister Alvira did their best to help take care of the two younger children, Alenza and Andrew, but his father realized that the children needed a mother. Francis Ladue soon remarried and his new wife took over the care of the children. Unfortunately, Joe seemed to resent his mother's replacement and did not respond well to her.

In 1868 Joe's father decided to move the family to Iowa. Joe, then fourteen years old did not want to go with them. He had never gotten along well with his stepmother and he loved the Adirondack Mountains. Reluctantly his father consented and arrangements were made for him to live with the James Henry Lobdell family on a neighboring farm. He would be able to help on the farm, attend school and continue his trapping and hunting. The Lobdells became his new family.

After finishing school Joe worked on the Lobdell farm and also did odd jobs here and there. He continued with his trapping and had acquired a small savings account. It was here that Joseph first met Katherine Mason, the young daughter of a neighboring family. Joe became very fond of Katherine, or Kitty" as she was called. He used to tell her stories and make her laugh. They became very good friends.

In 1879 Joe received word that his father had died. He traveled to Iowa to help settle his father's estate. It was there that he heard stories from his brother of fortunes being made in the goldfields in the Black Hills of South Dakota. He heard how General George Armstrong Custer had been an active developer of the project until he had been killed at the Little Bighorn three years ago. It occurred to Joe that here was a way for him to make a lot of money quickly .

Joe returned to Schuyler Falls and couldn't wait to tell the Lobdells of his plan. Earnestly he explained how fortunes were being made and that he knew he could make his. Joe had heard the gold siren and she called him to the Black Hills.

Shortly thereafter Joe showed up at the *Hidden Treasure Mine* near Deadwood, South Dakota. The foreman said that they weren't hiring miners, but he needed a man who could run a steam engine. Joe had never worked with steam engines, but he had at least seen the one in Mason's Saw Mill. He told the foreman that he could handle that just fine and was hired on the spot.

Somehow he figured things out and did very well. He spent his free time reading about mining methods and geology. Within a year Joe became foreman, and eighteen months later was promoted to superintendent of the mine. In his new position he earned a good salary and a small percentage. However, good things seldom last. A year later the mine was played out.

Joe returned to Schuyler Falls with a savings account of twelve hundred dollars. He told the Lobdells of the mining operation and thrilling accounts of life in a mining camp and in the notorious town of Deadwood.

After dinner Joe went over to the Mason's to visit Kitty. During the years he had been gone Kitty had bloomed into a beautiful young woman. She and Joe had come to realized that their friendship had become something much more meaningful and that they were deeply in love. Joe told her of his small fortune, and asked her to become his wife.

Bravely Joe approached Kitty's father and asked for her hand in marriage. Mr. Mason was not one to be impressed with a bank account of twelve hundred dollars. Joe was shocked to be so flatly rejected, for they had known each other for so long. The Masons, however, particularly Kitty's mother, considered Joe to be a penniless drifter, and totally unworthy of their daughter. The marriage was forbidden.

Joe told Kitty of his rejection, but already he had another plan. Joe knew mining now, and gold was to be found all over the west. There were new strikes in Wyoming and Colorado. Ever the optimist, Joe knew he would make it big. He asked her to please be patient and wait for him for just a few years. Then he would return for her and they could be wed.

Klondike Gold Rush Centennial Anthology

Kitty listened, hopefully. She had faith in Joe. She knew that he loved her, and that she loved him. Kitty promised she would wait, no matter how long it took.

Joe set out again for the West. This time it was Colorado, followed by Wyoming, New Mexico, Arizona and California. He was using up his cash but he still had enough for a stake in Alaska. He never doubted that he would strike it rich. Full of enthusiasm, he booked passage for the North, landing at Dyea, Alaska in June of 1882.

Dyea was at the foot of one of the only two glacier free passes that penetrate the sheer wall of the Pacific Coastal Range. This pass had been fiercely guarded by the Chilkoot Indians from time before memory. They controlled the trade between the white men and the Tagish Indians of the interior. It had been only the previous year that a U.S. Navy gunboat had persuaded the Chilkoots to allow white men free passage. Joe Ladue was one of the first to go through the, now famous, Chilkoot Pass unmolested by the Indians. He was even able to hire them as packers to help haul his gear over the 3,700 foot wall.

Joe prospected up and down the Yukon for the next six years, trying the Pelly River, the Stewart, the Fortymile, the Indian, the Klondike and several others. He would find enough gold to convince him that there was a large deposit somewhere in the Yukon Valley, but never enough to be called a strike.

In 1888 Joe set up near old Fort Selkirk, at a place then called Sixtymile. There was a trading post at Sixtymile operated by an old Irishman named Arthur Harper. Harper had come to the Yukon in 1873 and after prospecting a while, formed a trading company. He became partner to two other traders, Jack McQuesten and Al Mayo. They operated a string of posts all along the Yukon and extended easy credit to some two thousand prospectors in the area. The trio had an arrangement with the Alaska Commercial Company of San Francisco, and even owned their own steamboat on the river. Without the services and grubstaking by these three men, the Yukon could never have been prospected.

At Sixtymile Joe tried vegetable farming, raising potatoes, turnips, radishes, cabbage, barley and oats. Unfortunately, the Yukon growing season proved too short and his crop was destroyed by frost before it was harvested. Not one to be easily discouraged, Joe then set up a saw mill and began selling lumber to miners for their sluice boxes. The saw mill proved successful and Joe began to prosper.

It wasn't long before Harper realized that Joe and his sawmill would be a valuable addition to the firm of Harper, McQusten and Mayo. He invited Joe to become his partner at Sixtymile post. Joe accepted the offer. He knew that the big strike would come someday and there were more ways to get gold than by digging for it. When it came, he would be on the scene to provide the goods and services the miners would need.

One day, in 1893, a prospector named Robert Henderson and two companions came to Sixtymile. They had been prospecting unsuccessfully on the Pelly River for the past two years and were dead broke, discouraged, and ready to give up the whole thing. Joe, the perpetual optimist, spoke with Henderson. Of course Joe had prospected the Pelly and agreed that there was no gold to be found there. Nor was there, he said, any gold in the Stewart or the Klondike. He was certain, however, that the big strike would come, and that it would most likely be on the Indian River. Joe told Henderson he would grubstake him if he wanted to give it another try.

Henderson's two companions had had enough and decided to return to Colorado; but Henderson was overcome by Joe's enthusiasm and agreed to prospect the Indian River. Joe's share was to be fifty percent of whatever he found. For the next two years Henderson prospected the Indian River and its small tributaries or "pups." He found gold here and there, but never enough to satisfy him. Eventually he wandered over Solomon's Dome into the northern drainage, which is tributary to the Klondike River. Here he found the gold he was seeking, at least eight cents to the pan. (Two cents was considered good.)

Back over on the Indian River he persuaded three other men to join him on Gold Bottom Creek, as he had

Klondike Gold Rush Centennial Anthology

named it. By mid-summer of 1896 they had panned out about $800 worth of gold. It was time to go back to Sixtymile to tell Ladue and to reprovision. On his return trip from Sixtymile Henderson met George Carmack, a white man who had married an Indian woman and taken up Indian ways. Carmack was fishing at the mouth of the Klondike with his two brothers-in-law, Skookum Jim and Tagish Charlie. True to the miners' code, to spread the word of any new strike, Henderson told Carmack of his find and urged him to come up and stake on Gold Bottom. He added, however, "It's alright for you, George, but I don't want any dirty Siwash (Indians) stakin' on Gold Bottom." .

This offended Carmack and he declined to join Henderson. Instead the three men decided to prospect on nearby Rabbit Creek. A few days later, on August 16, 1896, they dipped up a four dollar pan. This was phenomenal . They soon had enough to fill an empty shotgun shell. George and Charlie set off down the river to Fortymile to file their claim, while Jim guarded the site and panned more gold. Everywhere George went he spread the word of his find. The only person he did not tell was Robert Henderson.

Joe Ladue got the word and realized that the strike he had been waiting for all these years had come at last. He set out for Fortymile to file his claim; not for a gold mine, but for a townsite at the mouth of the Klondike where it met the Yukon. On the way he met a man who wanted to buy lumber for a house on the Klondike. Being a shrewd businessman, Joe sent his claim on to Fortymile with a friend, while he returned to Sixtymile, dismantled his sawmill and floated it down to his new claim. On August 28th he landed at his new townsite and set up his saw mill. Soon there would be hundreds of houses at the new site, and Joe would sell the lumber for all of them.

He named the new town Dawson after a close friend, Dr. William Dawson, a prominent government geologist. Within two months a tent city of over two thousand prospectors bloomed on the flats of Dawson. Joe hired William Oglvie, the Canadian government surveyor, who surveyed the Alaskan-Canadian border, to survey the townsite and lay out building lots. Oglvie surveyed 160 acres for which Joe paid a government fee of $1.25 per acre. By January there were five houses in Dawson including Joe's. By May of 1897 Joe had a store and a saloon and building lots were selling for $5,000 apiece.

The winter of 1896-97 was a hard one in Dawson. Food was in short supply. The miners froze in their cabins and tents while mucking and digging through the deep permafrost to find the pay-streak. With spring came the breakup of the ice and the town was flooded. But eventually, in June, came the steamboat, *Alice*, with much needed supplies and dozens of barrels of whisky. Amid much celebration some eighty or so newly rich miners prepared to go "outside". The town went wild. Two days later the *Portus B. Weare* arrived with a similar cargo and the town went wild all over again.

Word arrived that Joe's partner, Arthur Harper, who had "gone outside" the year before for his health, had died in Arizona of tuberculosis. This saddened Joe for he was very fond of the old man. Harper had a reputation for honesty and had gained the complete trust and loyalty of the Indians. In a short time Joe Ladue had shared in that same trust and loyalty. He and Harper were a good team, and both prospered while waiting for the big day.

The *Alice* took aboard about forty outbound miners and started her return voyage to St. Michael. The *Weare* followed two days later with a similar number aboard. Among them was Joe Ladue, who was going back to Kitty Mason after an absence of fifteen years. In St. Michael Joe boarded the vessel *Excelsior*, bound for San Francisco. The *Portland*, bound for Seattle had sailed two days earlier with the miners from the *Alice*. These "goldships" would arrive in their respective ports on July 15th and 17th and set off the wildest stampede for gold the world had ever seen. The entire nation went mad with "Klondikeitis".

Joe Ladue and the returning miners were wined and dined and toasted by politician and financier alike. They were hounded and pursued by every kind of well-wisher, reporter, confidence man and schemer. For Joe, the same thing was repeated in Chicago and finally in Plattsburg,

Klondike Gold Rush Centennial Anthology

New York and Schuyler Falls.

Imagine the scene at the Lobdell farm. A bushel basket of mail awaited him with all kinds of offers and requests for endorsements. Friends and neighbors came to call. Strangers came to call. The dining room table was covered with gold nuggets and the visitors ooohed and aaahed. One can only imagine the reaction of Kitty's mother. Needless to say, Joe was now a very acceptable candidate for son-in-law.

Joe and Kitty were married on December 15, 1897. On their honeymoon they visited New York City and Washington, D.C., and were received at the White House by President and Mrs. McKinley.

They returned to New York and were joined by E.F. Botsford, a Plattsburg attorney. Here they formed and incorporated the *Joseph Ladue Gold Mining and Development Company*, with Joe as the President and Managing Director. A million dollars worth of stock was sold at one hundred dollars per share, with Joe as the principal stock holder. The company took over Joe's holdings in Dawson and eleven mines on the Bonanza Creek.

In March of 1898 Joe Ladue made a return trip to Dawson, accompanied by E.F. Botsford. Kitty went with him as far as San Francisco, where she remained with friends until his return in September. Also with him were two friends from Schuyler Falls, Ellis Turner and Willis LaMay. Turner remained in Dawson for the winter, working for Joe in his store.

Joe made another trip to Dawson the following spring. When he returned he found that Willis LeMay's wife was expecting a child. On December 16, 1899 she gave birth to a baby boy, but she died a short while later. Joe and Kitty adopted the baby, naming him Joseph Francis Ladue, after Joe's father.

Joe made one more trip to Dawson in the spring of 1900, but his health was beginning to fail. After returning he was diagnosed as having the same disease that had killed his old partner, Arthur Harper. In the fall he and Kitty traveled to Colorado where they hoped the dry air would restore him to health. He failed to improve. They returned to Schuyler Falls the following spring. Joe was extremely sick. His years in the extreme climate of the Yukon had taken their toll.

On June 27, 1901 Joseph Ladue died. In his lifetime he had known hardship and adversity, but his constant optimism and tenacity brought rich reward. He had known great adventure and success, and had helped bring about an event in our history of major importance. Fortune had briefly smiled, and he and Kitty had known happiness together.

BIBLIOGRAPHY

Adney, Tappan, *The Klondike Stampede*
Harper & Brothers Publishers, 1899, New York
UBC Press, 1994, Vancouver

Berton, Pierre, *The Klondike Fever*
Carroll & Craft Publishers, 1958, New York

Gates, Michael, *Gold at Fortymile Creek*
UBC Press, 1994, Vancouver

Johnson, James A. *Carmack of the Klondike*
Epicenter Press and Nordal & Schubart, 1990, Ganges, B.C.

Leonard, John W., *The Gold Fields of the Klondike*
London: T. Fisher Unwin, 1897, Chicago
Clairedge, 1994, Whitehorse

Martinsen, Ellen Lung, *Black Sand and Gold*
Binford & Mort Publishing, 1956, Portland

Spotswood, Ken, *Media Kit*
Yukon Anniversaries Commission, 1996, Whitehorse, Y.T.

Ladue, Joseph F. III, *Family Scrapbook*
Unpublished, Highlands, New York

Klondike Gold Rush Centennial Anthology

CATHARINE CLARK-SAYLES • SAN RAFAEL, CALIFORNIA

Single Jack

I am a good man with a single jack,
I ain't tall, but down here tall ain't good
Crack your head on a stope
And you got better air down low.

Bad air, cave-in, water where it ain't
Supposed to be, steam pockets hissing
Like a snake out to eat your face,
Scald your face right off.

Not a week goes by you don't lose a friend
To the hole, and if the hole
Don't get him the consumption will,
In the deep holes, three or four thousand feet

What you breathe ain't air
Black stink, hot and wet
Scorch your lungs right out.
Down deep a man works in his skin

Like he was born, swings steel
Like fury, fifteen minutes a shift
One hundred and forty degrees
Crawling along the ceiling of Hell,

One day we're gonna break through
Instead of gold quartz find brimstone fires
And Old Nick toasting souls
On a marshmallow stick.

You gasp to the bucket, push an iron cart
Popping like a griddle
Mucking up high grade, cloudy quartz
With gleaming gold thread.

Mother lode is a secret
The earth is not gonna tell easy.
When you climb in the bucket, pull in tight,
Leave an arm poking out careless

Klondike Gold Rush Centennial Anthology 41

And you lose it quick
Caught deep in the earth
Between rock walls and a bucket of gold.
Don't matter it's winter above with ice

And snow, below it's Hell-hot
And a man can't work more'n a quarter hour
Before he's got to pull up gulping
Ice water and air like a dying trout,

Then back to the hole twelve hours a day
There's miles of timbers down there
Holding back miles of earth
Every tree for three hundred miles

Gone into the hole, into square-sets,
They ain't green they're
Creosote-black from the candles
We wear like an eye on our head,

When the earth shifts, they groan
Sometimes they shiver and snap,
Sometimes they don't hold and the earth
Rumbles back, then

It don't matter how good a man is
With a single jack, don't matter
How much gold he's got,
If he can't run fast he's gonna stay down

In the hole, in the deep, in the black.

The S.S. Excelsior

The Ship With the Golden Whistle

A story from the life of Captain Daniel B. Hutchings.

T he brass pipes of the *S.S. Excelsior*'s steam whistle
were polished to shine like gold. When she blew one
long, one short, one long, the company signal for arrival
or departure sure, she sang to me like the mating call of
some exotic sea bird.

But to the would-be prospectors and fast buck artists
in Seattle her musical whistle signaled gold. They milled
around the ship like flies around sugar. Every man Jack of
them expected to make a quick fortune in the Alaskan
gold rush and couldn't wait to get up to the Territory. As I
went about my duties as second mate I heard talk of
"strikes", "digs", "trades" and "stakes". And when I was
around these men I could smell the lust for gold.

The steamship was loaded to the scuppers with cargo
to be shipped north. Mining equipment, tools, food, dogs,
horses and cattle. Her passenger list included soldiers
headed for the army barracks in Kodiak and one lone
female schoolteacher. The *Excelsior* was the second ship of
the Pacific Steam Whaling Company's fleet of former
whalers still with their masts intact although their sails
had given way to the mighty steam engines installed
below decks.

The year was 1899 and I was on board on my first
assignment as a ship's officer for I had finally reached the
advanced age of eighteen.

Our first port of call was to be Juneau in the Alaskan
Territory where we expected to unload most of the
prospectors. We steamed out of Puget Sound and into the
Inside Passage without incident. The *Excelsior* seemed to
run herself which was a great difference from working a
ship under sail where every member of the crew had to be
ready to jump every hour of the day and night—as I had
for the past three years aboard sailing ships.

By actual count we had on board one hundred first

class passengers, one hundred and forty steerage passengers, and sharing their quarters below decks, twenty horses, fifteen cows and thirty dogs, animals of great value in the fragile land to the North where so few live things could breed.

With this cargo, we were loaded so deeply we had little reserve buoyancy and proceeded up the Coast more slowly than Chief Engineer Quinn had predicted.

At midnight on our fifth day out of Seattle we entered the Gastineau Canal out of Juneau. The warm, yellow glow of the city's lights could be seen through the fog off our bow. We were to land in Juneau in about twenty minutes.

At the sound of four bells, I went below to my cabin to get into my oilskins to prepare for a wet landing.

I had one heavy weather boot pulled on when a lurch of the ship threw me to the port side and I hit the washbowl. My forehead struck one of the metal faucets. I pulled on the other boot in a hurry to get out of the cabin for I knew we had hit something.

Irish, the first mate, was standing at the foot of the ladder, urging the crew up to the deck. When he saw me he took a look at my forehead.

"Goddam it, Dan," he barked, "This is no time to hurt yourself, I think we've hit a growler. Up the ladder man!"

On deck the word went around, the S.S. *Excelsior* had hit an iceberg, one of the low submerged bergs so hard to see at night, a "growler".

From the bridge Captain Downing shouted orders while the pilot stood behind him at the wheel looking stunned .

"You Dan, uncover the lifeboats—throw out the cargo, quick now!"

Coal oil, boxed fruit and vegetables stored in the lifeboats because of our shortage of space were thrown furiously into the water and on to the decks. I hadn't even had a chance to see the iceberg we'd hit because I was so busy sliding crates across the decks.

The passengers watched us working to free the lifeboats from the davits, but didn't seem to grasp the fact that our ship was in trouble. The *Excelsior* wasn't listing and the lights of Juneau still shone invitingly ahead.

Irish worked beside me as we at last swung the lifeboats free and ready to lower if need be. He said, "The Captain just came on deck, not fifteen minutes ago, he's the one that sighted the berg."

"What about the pilot?" I said, "that's what he was hired to do."

Irish spat in the water far below, "That pilot gave the engine room the signal for full astern, hard aport, thinking we would miss the berg, I guess, but Cap'n Downing yelled "no!" and told the helmsman not to move the wheel. "Steady as you go," he says, the very next second we hit the berg bow on right square on her stem."

With my four years at sea behind me I knew that the pilot's instruction for hard aport would have meant that the ship would strike the berg behind the collision bulkhead and water would have entered the ship's hull, probably sinking us. The Captain's order to strike the berg bow on allowed the watertight bulkhead in the bow to keep the rushing water from entering the ship's hull—at least for now.

I looked up at the Captain barking orders. Behind his back the crew said he was deaf, but now it seemed he wasn't deaf, but only heard what he wanted to hear.

The two hundred and forty passengers had all come up on deck and were bunched together in a crowd below us. They were all dressed and ready to disembark and go prospecting. Because the engines had stopped they thought we were making port. Hitting the berg was a minor incident they could tell the folks back home about.

Old John Barleycorn was keeping them warm and oblivious.

They were so unconcerned, I would have stopped worrying myself, except for the grey blue pieces of iceberg I saw floating in the water around us and except for the noises coming from the horses down in steerage.

One was whinnying like a spooked horse and when she stopped the dogs would fill in with wild yips. Animals sensed danger a lot faster than people did. I began to feel

Klondike Gold Rush Centennial Anthology 45

just a little afraid for our ship.

The schoolteacher came up to me as I stood by the lifeboats and asked me why we had hit an iceberg.

I assumed my best second officer manner and told her, "M'am, the growlers, as we sailors call them, are so low in the water, so dull colored—just like the sea, and so barely awash no human eye could see them at night."

She pulled her sealskin cape more tightly around her little body and said, "I thought the Pacific Steam Whaling Company had better navigators, or I wouldn't have taken this ship. I will report this incident to my brother as soon as I set foot in Juneau."

Her brother was the all church missionary in Juneau. That didn't impress me too much but I did agree with the little lady that the Pacific Steam Whaling Company might have better pilots.

It was funny that no one else seemed to hear or notice the sound of the horses whinnying below, but it was beginning to unnerve me. I was about to ask permission to go below and check the animals when Captain Downing shouted at me.

"Uncover the searchlight, get it ready!"

I thought the Captain intended using the light to spot the Juneau docks. As I unlaced the canvas cover of the light I heard the speaking tube whistle blow from the engine room. Captain and pilot ran to the chart house to hear what Chief Engineer Quinn had to say from the engine room. I reached the chart house just in time to see Captain Downing throw down the tube and give the engine room one bell to start the engines slow ahead.

I heard him say to the pilot, "Where's the nearest beach to put her on?"

The plump, blond-bearded pilot once more appeared to lose his power to think.

"Hurry, you damned fool, we've got to get her beached now!" The captain yelled the now.

The pilot came out of his dream, "About two miles on the port hand is the closest place to beach her."

The Captain whistled down the tube, "How long can we keep steam up, Quinn?"

I heard the engineer's faraway voice saying, "Not more than ten minutes, Captain."

Captain Downing spotted me. "Ten minutes to get her beached, or we swim for it."

Pictures raced through my mind of two hundred and forty people swimming in those icy waters along with the horses, cows and dogs. We were short two lifeboats for that size crowd, let alone survival for the animals. The gold fever had led the company to load beyond the capacity to handle emergencies. And the horses still wailed in steerage.

I had to push back panic now and remind myself that I was an officer on this stricken ship . I knew that only the Captain, the pilot, the engineer and myself knew of the real danger .

Irish was directing the passengers and the rest of the crew aft of the ship. Everyone thought they would be safely landed in Juneau within thirty minutes.

And I knew that we had only ten minutes to keep the ship afloat, not even enough time to load and lower the lifeboats.

Rapidly, the Captain confided to me that the fireroom was filling because the collision bulkhead had now collapsed. There was only enough steam left in the big boiler to operate the triple expansion engines for ten minutes more.

The Captain turned and whistled down the tube, then said, "Full ahead, Mr. Quinn."

To me he snapped, "Relieve the sailor at the wheel and keep her hard over to port. Ride her straight onto the beach. I will be standing right behind you," he paused, "And so will the pilot".

I ran for the wheel and relieved the able seaman, Scotty. I told him, "Take that searchlight, direct her high beam in front of the ship to the port side. For God's sake watch out for any more growlers, or rocks. We're riding this baby right onto the nearest beach."

Scotty didn't ask questions. He jumped for the searchlight and switched her on high beam. As the beam of light shot high over the water, silence at last overcame the passengers on deck. I could still hear the horse whinnying below.

In my hands the wheel went hard over and steady. I could actually hear Captain Downing and the pilot behind me breathing on my neck.

A little to the right and the Captain whispered, "Steady as she goes, you're on course."

I felt the engines straining full speed ahead as I gripped the wheel so hard I could see my knuckles turning white.

The Captain breathed in my ear, "Five minutes to go, Mister."

"Aye, aye, Sir," I muttered.

Directly ahead the searchlight was picking up the rocks of a dark beach. The ship shuddered as the engines suddenly stopped. We rocked from side to side as our momentum carried us about a hundred feet up over the beach until we ground to a stop with a sickening crunch.

The passengers were screaming. I hung onto the wheel which was shimmying with the shock as the ship listed over to her port side. Then I calmly reached into my pants pocket and pulled out the gold watch I had inherited from my Dad. The watch had stopped with the impact, the hands pointed to two thirty five. We had arrived in exactly ten minutes.

The Captain and pilot clung to each other behind me. Then the Captain let go of his nemesis and reached up to blow the golden whistle. One long, one short, one long, the signal that meant arrival. On the last pull she ran out of steam.

At the sound of the whistle the passengers quieted down but the dogs began to howl, but no sound from the whinnying horses. Either they were worn out or at last felt safe.

But now in a quick, ugly change of mood the passengers were beginning to move toward Captain Downing. They lurched over the canted deck toward the three of us at the wheel waving whiskey bottles and cursing the Captain, the pilot and that little guy at the wheel who had wrecked the ship.

 Klondike Gold Rush Centennial Anthology

They moved in a mass toward us, shouting about their cargo. None of them had been physically injured. Apparently the only injury aboard was my own goose egg swelling on my forehead.

The crew came running up to form a ring around the three of us and Captain Downing's granite face took on a humorous look as he stood there, at an angle, listening to the passenger's complaints.

After five minutes of listening to the clamor, he wrapped his blue wool scarf twice around his long turkey neck, straightened the cap with gold braid and deliberately walked away from the crowd to his cabin below.

As he left I took it upon myself to make a little speech. I looked down at the angry faces of the drunks who were now suddenly sobering and said, "Listen you fools, put down those bottles and listen! If it hadn't been for Captain Downing we would all be frozen in the water half an hour ago. The fireroom was filling with water from the collision with the berg, beaching this ship saved your lives and your cargo!!"

The dogs howled agreement from steerage. I repeated, "Beaching this ship saved all of our lives!" and staggered off the bridge, for I was exhausted.

Now the horses whinnied again and at the sound the crowd laughed. Irish came up and took my arm to keep me steady.

"Go back to your quarters and pack to disembark immediately. That means right now" he bellowed, "we'll take the animals and cargo off the ship tomorrow."

The lady school teacher was plucking at his sleeve, "but how will we get off the ship?" she squeaked.

He told her gently, "You'll find ladders over the side in a few minutes, then we'll be taking a moonlight hike together into the town."

The first mile of our hike along the beach toward Juneau was lightened by the jovial spirits of some of the younger men. As we started the second mile some of our passengers stumbled and had to be helped to their feet and then the grumbling began again. Irish brought up the rear with the woman and tried to quiet everyone down.

Klondike Gold Rush Centennial Anthology

Captain Downing, the pilot and I led the crowd along the rocky beach. The reserved Captain seemed lost in thought. I felt a great sympathy for him because it was a captain's duty to keep his ship safely in the water and now this captain's vessel was smashed on the beach. I had been the one to steer the ship there but the captain was responsible. If he had reached the bridge sooner, spotted the iceberg sooner, would we still be safely in deep water? And yet, he made no word of complaint to the pilot.

I wanted to praise the Captain for his foresight in striking the berg head on instead of swinging away from it as the pilot had instructed. When I started to speak to him he turned unhappily away. Some of the passengers tried to question him about the safety of their supplies and animals. He just said "It will be all right, it will be all right" and kept walking over the rocks toward the town ahead of us.

It took us almost two hours to make that walk into Juneau. I found the cannery superintendent and he gave us permission to take our crowd into the empty bunk houses where we all could sleep on the bare floors. As I finally lay down to sleep on the wooden planks my last fervent thought was the hope that I would never be in command of a beached ship.

I woke to see Captain Downing standing over me, the toe of his boot gently nudging my shoulder. He appeared clean shaven and neatly dressed, his cap square on his head, his boots shining. Obviously, Captain Downing had not slept in the past hour.

While the rest of the crew and the passengers continued to sleep, the Captain, Chief Engineer Quinn and I took a little fishing dory from the beach. We pushed her off and headed for the *S.S. Excelsior*.

As the junior officer, I automatically sat down to row the dory, the Captain sat down in front of me and Mr. Quinn on the slat behind me. It was still too dark to see so I rowed by compass to the south where the *Excelsior* lay on the beach. Quinn and the Captain talked of the salvage of the ship. Quinn was to check the engine room for temporary repair and inspect the collision bulkhead forward. The Captain would inspect the rest of the ship and I was to see to the animals and feed them.

I knew I would have to hear those cows and horses and dogs crying and bellowing as though they blamed me for the wreck. I would listen to them, clean them up and feed them with compassion. Poor, dumb animals, they trusted me, for I was a human being.

I rowed on through the night listening to the remarks being exchanged over my head.

"You thought that fancy steam engine of yours would never give up, Quinn." The Captain tamped his pipe full of damp tobacco from a greasy leather pouch.

Quinn, cursing gently under his breath, leaned over my shoulder and struck match after match trying to light the Captain's pipe.

When the tobacco finally flared up with a small light in the darkness, the Captain continued, "You can't beat a good sailing ship for a mind of her own. As long as there's one mast left, she'll stay afloat and sail."

I whispered a quiet "amen" to that.

He puffed on the pipe and I could see his face lit up as he put another match to the pipe. He puffed reflectively, "But take a steamship now, when her engines stop, her heart stops and she'll die. Without those engines she's a lost ship, stranded, high and dry."

Behind me, I heard Quinn laugh and spit into the water. "You can't outwit the sea Cap'n, not on any kind of a ship. We'll get those engines back in shape and the fire-room pumped out today. Tomorrow, we'll have the whole crew at work on the bulkhead. A week from now we'll be moving into Seattle under our own steam. You'll see."

The next day some three hundred men, most of our passengers and the population of Juneau turned out to help us repair and refloat the *Excelsior*. They brought pulleys, cranes and donkey engines over the rocky beach or rowed them over by boat. One of the deepwater ships in the harbor steamed over close to us and stood by to assist in the remarkable job of refloating the *Excelsior* as soon as temporary repairs were made.

Mr. Quinn was right. Within three days, working day

and night, we had the cargo unloaded and the repairs made. We steamed out of Juneau and headed down the Inside Passage under our own power to drydock in Seattle.

When we entered the port of Seattle under slow bell we were met by the familiar little tugboats and pushed toward the drydock. As the ship bumped the pier, I stood by to blow the golden whistle signaling arrival; one long, one short, one long.

A crowd had gathered on the dock to the see the ship that had hit an iceberg, been beached, and now, floated again.

The lines were tied and I blew the whistle signaling arrival. Then I blew it again, the crowd didn't know it, but with the second signal, I paid my respects to Captain Downing.

CHRISTINE SCHMITZ · GAINSVILLE, FLORIDA

Klondike Woman

for M. J. Mayer

Ignore the diminutive particulars,
The crude morgues and cities of canvas.
No trail will differ from the next.

Flotillas of colonization limp north: sloops,
Barques, and scows, where nations of ice
Crack into water. Even they will prove too little.

A Ton of Gold started this gold rush not you.
So abandon the silent lodging of your pass,
Where the rains stretch down like prison bars,

And the oxen rot in mudholes.
Bear up the search. Carry us like stones
In your pocket when you step into water.

And when you make it,
Sack up the gold like wheat.
Like wheat, take as much of it with you.

Then tomorrow, write home to tell us *it's true*,
No one telling anyone what to do, everyone doing.
And the gold...

Woman, here is your pick and your shovel.
Unearth what you can.

JOHN W. WASHBURN • NORTHVILLE, NEW YORK

To Find Yukon Gold

On the night of September 28th I found myself on board the Motor Vessel Malaspina, bound for Skagway, Alaska. At last I was going to climb the dreaded Chilkoot Pass myself, and see what the stampeders saw one hundred years ago. I had flown out of Seattle the day before and spent the night in Juneau. Now I was bound for the Chilkoot by way of the Marine Highway ferry, on the "red-eye" run between Juneau and Skagway. I had come aboard at midnight and should arrive in Skagway around 8:00 AM.

I thought of the stampeders of 1897 who traveled this same route, but under much more difficult circumstances. Every old scow that would float, steam or sail was pressed into service to cash in on the vast horde of gold-crazed chechakos. They were stacked up four deep on hastily constructed wooden bunks in the hold, or crowded on deck exposed to the elements. They were fed barely palatable food, in rotating shifts, or else had to feed themselves from their packs. When they arrived at Dyea they were dumped into the shallow water to wade ashore. Their outfits were lightered ashore and dumped on the beach, frequently ruined by an incoming tide. I marveled at their unflinching determination to get to the gold fields.

I thought of my grandfather. He had joined the stampede to the Yukon in 1897. He went over the Chilkoot that winter and made it all the way to Dawson City in the spring. He found that all the good claims had already been staked and filed by men who had been in the Yukon before the discovery. He had gone to work for wages on Eldorado number 5 for a miner named Frank Keller. The wages had been good, and he came out with $1,200 and a large nugget in June of 1899. The money didn't last, but he had worn that nugget around his neck, like a badge of honor, for the rest of his life.

As our ship drew nearer to Skagway I could see the town, its streets laid out in straight lines before me. Beyond the town I could see the White Pass, extending like a giant notch cut out of the solid wall of rock that rose steeply on all sides. The Skagway River, flowing down from the pass, enters the Lynn Canal at this point. In 1897-98 over three thousand horses and mules were killed by overwork and neglect, to move some five thousand stampeders through the pass to the headwaters. In 1899 the White Pass Railroad was completed, linking Skagway to the Yukon, assuring the town's survival.

Another mile or so to the north, the Taiya River enters the Lynn Canal. That is where the town of Dyea was located one hundred years ago. It was the port of entry for the Chilkoot Pass. Prior to the completion of the White Pass Railroad, the Chilkoot was the preferred route. It was higher, but some twelve miles shorter than the White Pass Route. The Chilkoot Indians, who controlled the Pass, had been permitting whitemen to use it since the early 1880s. With the completion of the White Pass Railroad, however, Dyea ceased to exist. Today scarcely a board is left standing where a town of twenty thousand once stood.

I landed in Skagway around 8:30 AM. I hired a taxi to take me over the winding nine mile road to Dyea, and the trailhead of the Chilkoot. I paid the cab driver and he wished me luck. He had explained to me that the trail had been officially closed for the past two weeks. The Park Service rangers and the Parks Canada wardens, who provide oversight and safety services were no longer on duty. Some people still hike the trail during the winter months, but he didn't think I should try it by myself.

I acknowledged his advice, but assured him that I would be alright. I had done a lot of solo hiking in New York's Adirondack Mountains and I had planned this trip very carefully. Of course I had never seen the Chilkoot Pass before, but that was the whole point. I wanted to see the pass without being accompanied by a couple hundred tourist hikers. I not only wanted to see it, I wanted to experience it, to feel it, to become a part of it...!

About a mile from the trailhead is the Slide Cemetery. On April 3, 1898, Palm Sunday, a deadly avalanche roared off the south wall of the pass just above Sheep Camp. Nearly one hundred men and women were trapped by the slide, but many were dug out alive by rescuers. My grandfather had been one of them.

In all, sixty-eight stampeders lost their lives. Some of them were probably friends of my grandfather. Most of the dead were buried in the *Slide Cemetery* near Dyea. I had planned to visit the site before hiking the trail, but did not want to take the time to walk the extra two miles, over and back. I decided to put it off until after the trip.

I left the trailhead and started up the trail. Almost immediately the ground rose up steeply and wound its way around switchbacks and boulders as I climbed through a northern rain forest of spruce and alder. I hadn't expected so steep a rise and found I had to stop to catch my breath rather frequently. I estimate I climbed about five hundred feet in a distance of a quarter mile. Then after about half a mile of smaller ups and downs the trail descended just as sharply right back down to the level of the Taiya River. It was quite an introduction to the Chilkoot. "*At least*, I thought, *it can't get much tougher than that*".

The trail was easier going after that, joining an old wagon road. After a few miles I passed an old sawmill site, marked by a tumbling down shack, some assorted pieces of machinery and a huge sawdust pile. A little further on I came to Finnigan's point, where there was a shelter tent frame and an outhouse. It seemed like a good place to stop for lunch. Looking across the river I could watch a white ribbon of water cascading down from Irene Glacier at the top of the mountain.

After lunch the trail went up and down and crisscrossed a small channel of the Taiya on a series of small foot bridges, before climbing a few hundred feet, only to descend again through the most fascinating moss covered forest I had ever seen. In a short time a well weathered cabin came into view and I knew I had reached the Canyon Shelter, my home for the night. The cabin was not here during the gold rush. It was built in the 1960s by State of Alaska trail crews. It was, however, a welcome sight, as the weather had clouded up and a misty drizzle was in the air.

I was impressed. Here I was, at last, in a cabin in

Klondike Gold Rush Centennial Anthology

Alaska on the Chilkoot Trail, at least eight miles from the nearest human being. I loved the feeling of solitude; drinking hot coffee, sitting on the front porch, in a rocking chair that someone had chainsaw carved out of a single chunk of wood. As I sat and sipped, I could almost sense the ghosts of the stampeders. I wondered, had someone sat here a hundred years ago and sipped, as he dreamed golden daydreams?

The next morning, after a breakfast of plain oatmeal and coffee, I started up the trail. Soon I came to the swing bridge that crosses over to the former site of Canyon City. In 1898 it was a community of 1,500 people, complete with electricity. It housed a couple dozen businesses including hotels, saloons, outfitting stores, restaurants and at least one brothel. It was the head of navigation for boats or wagons, and power station for the tramway that ran seven miles to the summit. With the completion of the White Pass Railway in 1899, Canyon City, like Dyea, simply vanished.

Bypassing Canyon City, I began the climb out of the canyon. There was a long set of steps that had been dug into the steep hillside. It wound around a switchback and ended at the top on an open rock surface. From this vantage point I could look back down the valley and see the Lynn Canal, nearly ten miles away.

I continued on and passed Pleasant Camp by midmorning and reached Sheep Camp by noon. In the winter of 1898 this community provided all kinds of goods and services to some 8,000 transients at any given time. By spring it too vanished, as the horde had moved on to Lakes Lindeman and Bennett.

The mountain ridge to the east, that parallels the river, rises steeply some 4,000 feet like a rock wall. Numerous waterfalls poured off its side and streamed on down to the river. Just two years ago, a spring avalanche had roared down this mountain and obliterated the old camping area, one mile above the present site. As I passed through that area I could still see sizable tree trunks that had been snapped off eight to ten feet above the ground, the tops all lay pointing down slope. They testified both to the depth of the snow at the time, and the tremendous power and energy of an avalanche.

My plan was to camp at the foot of the pass, so I pushed on, entering an area known as Long Hill. It is well named, for in the next three miles it rises continuously for another two thousand five hundred feet. After passing the timberline I encountered a vast field of skree (large boulders) that covered the mountainside and extended all the way to the roaring glacial stream that was the beginning of the Taiya River. I was forced to climb atop the boulders and rock-hop from one to the next for about one hundred yards. This was the site of the great avalanche of 1898 that had killed sixty-eight goldseekers. It gave me an eerie feeling, like walking through a graveyard on a dark night.

After leaving the skree field I soon came to another rather steep section. There was actually a path worn on it and it switched back and forth. What was left of the stream had disappeared to the right, as I climbed away from it. Soon the trail leveled, and stretched out before me for about a quarter mile. I had reached the area known as the Scales, and rising before me was what appeared to be a vertical field of scree, the *Golden Stairs*. The most stirring image of the gold rush was a stark picture of this slope, snow covered, with an unbroken line of heavily burdened men climbing straight up, in virtual lock-step, to the sky.

In 1897-98 some enterprising packers had actually cut steps into the ice and snow that covered the scree. This made it easier to climb the 45 degree pitch that rose another eight hundred feet to the summit. It would take hours for a man to make the climb with fifty to a hundred pounds on his back, and few could make more than one trip per day. The stampeders had to make thirty to forty trips to move their two thousand pound outfits to the summit. It's no wonder the over half of the stampeders turned back when confronted with the *Chilkoot Pass*.

I set up my tent right at the foot of the *Golden Stairs*, on the small snow field that remained from the previous winter. It may have been cold, but it was more comfortable than the rocks. I boiled my freeze-dried dinner and

Klondike Gold Rush Centennial Anthology

made some coffee. Looking around, I realized that I had never felt so all alone, and yet I didn't feel quite alone. It was a strange, paradoxical feeling.

I slept fitfully. The wind was blowing up the canyon from the Lynn Canal, bringing with it moisture, which condensed into a mist. I could hear the wind howling through the rocks and shivered at the sound. At this point I came to regret all the warm, comforting coffee I had drunk the previous evening. It was only four o'clock and I had to leave my warm sleeping bag, and my dry tent, to venture out into the elements. Nature can be cruel.

As I was returning to my tent, anticipating my cozy sleeping bag, I thought I saw something moving through the mist in the morning half light. As I stared into the darkness a figure emerged from the wind blown mist. Then I saw other figures behind him. They were all bent over under heavy loads on their backs. Their numbers grew until I could make out the forms of fifty or sixty individuals. They were all dressed in a similar fashion; wool or fur caps with ear flaps, Mackinaw coats, and high-top leather boots. (I hadn't seen boots like those since I was a boy.)

Their faces were drawn and they all looked worn out. I wondered who they could be and what they were doing wandering about on the mountain at this hour. It was all very strange and I felt more than a little apprehension.

The first one drew closer to me and he spoke. His voice had a strange, hollow sound to it. "Hello, stranger", he said. "Have you been sent to join us?"

"Join you?" I questioned. "Who are you?" Why are you climbing the Chilkoot in the middle of the night? Where did you come from?" As I spoke I looked more closely at him and suddenly realized that I was looking right through him. My apprehension changed to fear, and was fast approaching downright terror.

"Don't be alarmed," he reassured me. "I didn't realize... You're the first living soul we've seen in a long time. We mean you no harm."

"Wh-wh-who are you? I demanded; sounding more sure of myself than I really was.

"The name is Eli, Eli Erlanger," he replied. That's short for Eliphalet. Who are you?"

"My name is Venner, Jason Venner," I answered. Then his words registered. "What did you mean, I'm the first living soul you've seen...?

"Hmmm," he interrupted, "I knew a Jason Venner back in '98. Came up from Dyea with him"

"What do you mean, back in '98. This is '97; ...and what did you mean by first living soul?" I was really getting nervous at this point.

His expression changed to one of concern. "Now look stranger, don't get upset, and don't be afraid, but what I meant was 1897; and you are the first living soul we have seen in years. You see, we're all dead. We died in the big avalanche back in April of 1898"

"You've got to be kidding! Do you expect me to believe...?"

"Son!" He hesitated. "Look at me. Look at all of us. Don't we look a little different to you? Believe me, this is no jest."

You mean you're really...? All of you...? And we're talking? How can...?"

"I don't know Mr. Venner, but here we are; sixty-eight of us! We were suffocated in the snow slide. Most of us are buried down in Dyea, but all of us are here in spirit." he concluded.

I had to believe my senses. "But why," I asked, "are you here?"

"I guess it's because of our lust for gold," he answered. "We wanted to be the first to the goldfields. We were warned about the danger of an avalanche, but we wouldn't listen. Even the Indian packers refused to work that day. We should have known... but we wanted to get over the pass." He paused. "Now we are doomed to climb this cursed pass every night, until we find Yukon gold. The trouble is that we never get to the summit. How can we ever find the gold?"

"And you have been doing this for almost one hundred years? I asked.

"Yep! and from the looks of things, we'll be doing it

Klondike Gold Rush Centennial Anthology

forever."

I had recovered my composure, yet it was still hard to accept that I was standing there talking to a specter. I hadn't believed in such things. "Mr. Erlanger," I began, "You said you knew a Jason Venner back in '97. That man had to have been my grandfather. He was buried in the same avalanche in which all of you died, but he was dug out alive. I want you to know that he never forgot you and the others. He talked about that day for the rest of his life."

"I figured he lived through it," Eli said, "when he wasn't here with us. I'm glad to hear he made it. Got married and raised a family eh? Did he ever strike it rich in the goldfields?"

"No! Not really," I answered. "He mined for wages and did fairly well. He did bring back some gold too." Then an idea hit me. "Hey! That may be the answer to your problem.

"I don't understand what you mean," Eli said. "How could that be the answer to...?"

"Because," I interrupted the ghost, "He wore a large gold nugget around his neck until just before he died. On his death bed he gave it to me and I now wear it. It's Yukon gold." I opened my collar and removed the large nugget for all to see.

The entire company of specters gasped as one. Then as it dawned on them what this meant, they all cheered, "Gold! Yukon gold! We have found Yukon gold!"

I can honestly say that I have never seen so many happy dead guys.

"Jason," Eli spoke, "do you realize what this means? (I nodded). "You've freed us from a hundred year old curse. Tonight we will be able to reach the summit and our spirits will be free at last.

He tried to shake my hand, but his hand passed right through mine. We gotta go now, "he said, "but I will speak well of you to your grandfather when I see him. Goodbye, Jason Venner, and thank you."

The line of sixty-eight was moving off without a sound. They didn't climb over the boulders, but rather climbed as though they were on stairs chopped into the ice and snow. Only there was no ice and snow. Silently, they moved up the *Golden Stairs*; sixty-eight ghastly, grinin' ghosts, turning and waving back to me as they climbed into the mist of the early dawn.

Eli was the last in the long line and I watched them go. "Yes!" I thought out loud, "they would reach the summit this time. "As one by one, they disappeared over the first false summit Eli turned. He stared back down the slope and waved one last time. Then he too was gone. The silence was profound. I realized that the Klondike Gold Rush was finally over.

I awoke around 8:00 AM in my sleeping bag. For a moment I didn't realize where I was. Then it came back to me, the sixty-eight specters. Except that it was very vivid, and clear in my mind, not like most dreams. I remembered Eli Erlander and the ghostly company. It had all been so strange, but it seemed so real.

I pressed on and went all the way to Bare Loon Lake that day. The next day I hiked out to Log Cabin and caught the van that runs from Whitehorse to Skagway. All the way back the memory of my dream had haunted me and stayed with me. I knew it was only a dream, but still I felt I had to go back to Dyea to visit the *Slide Cemetery*.

The taxi took me right to the cemetery entrance. I asked him to wait for me. The cemetery was located in the woods. Off to the left was a small private cemetery and the markers revealed that these were the graves of native Americans. Some of them were very old.

A short way further there was a little gate that led to a larger burial ground. The markers were randomly arranged among the trees and weeds that had grown up. The markers were in poor condition. Each one bore the name of the deceased and the state from which he came. Each one bore the inscription, *"Died April 3, 1898."*

Being here made my dream seem all the more real. Even though I had never heard of any of these men, it seemed as though I knew them. It was very strange. As I was about to leave I noticed one other marker that I had missed when I entered. It read:

Klondike Gold Rush Centennial Anthology

JOHN W. WASHBURN • NORTHVILLE, NEW YORK

ELI ERLANGER

Michigan

Died April 3, 1898

R.I.P.

The Gold Rush was finally over.

ANTHONY RUSSELL WHITE • HILLSBOROUGH, CALIFORNIA

A Poem For John Renshaw

Quick! You're young again, John.
Get on your sturdy raft—push off!
A mighty milky silt-laden river
surges by your brandnew boots,
past soaring stands of red cedars,
a gravel bar where three deer drink,
past a sunrise-brightened cliff face—
perhaps it's the gold-swollen Yukon.

Later I want to hear everything!
Over heaps of white salmon bones
around a dying alder-wood campfire,
with the sticky fishskin shining silver
on your fingers, you will gesture—
the wingspan of that eagle,
the shape of that rapids,
the height of that bear,
the number of stars
on that brief
moon-less
night.

HOPE MORRITT • POINT EDWARD, ONTARIO, CANADA

GOLD DIGGERS

There were many famous gold diggers in the Klondike of 1897-98, but none more famous (or infamous) than the dance hall girls—and they, like hundreds of miners, often found fool's gold.

The dance hall girl was like the movie actress of a much later era. But—in those early years in Dawson, she did not enjoy the exalted position of a movie queen. Strict Victorian ethics put her at the bottom of the social scale—a notch above a prostitute—and yet, she was more visible and colorful than her "sinful" sister. Also—hardened miners showered her with gold and a tinsel kind of love.

Lime Juice Lil was a talented dancer at *The Orpheum*, an elite Dawson theater. Gowned in ankle-length silk with a diaphanous cape, she was famous for free-flowing movements that highlighted her interpretative dance numbers. After several performances on stage each night, she donned a plain blouse and ankle-length skirt, and, as a hostess, danced with the men who hugged a bar in a nearby room. Here, like many dance hall entertainers, she became a "percentage girl", reaping a 25% commission on each drink a man ordered. Beer, whiskey and gin cost a dollar a shot, and champagne was sold by the bottle at sixty dollars a quart. The percentage girl kept the corks from the champagne bottles and cashed in on them after the saloon closed.

Lil drank only lime juice so she knew exactly what she was doing when she got a man drunk and "rolled" him. She left *The Orpheum* with a lot more than percentage money from drinks.

The North West Mounted Police were well aware of Lil's notorious activities, and when they got the goods on her they sent her a summons to appear before the Commissioner. She knew she'd get a blue ticket—the ultimate in punishment, an escort to the outside world, and no back-tracking, or she'd go to prison.

Lil was worried and asked to see the Commissioner alone, prior to her appearance. Dressed in a conservative tweed suit, her pretty face the essence of innocence, she explained that she was in love with a waiter and was pregnant with his child and they planned to be married. The Commissioner told her to come to see him the next day, with her waiter, and when they appeared he hurried them over to a nearby mission church where the minister stood ready to marry them. A child never appeared, but, as the Mountie had hoped, Lil gave up the theater for the more mundane duties of a house wife.

The Yukon gold rush began on August 17th, 1896 when a squawman—George Washington Carmack, and his in-laws, Skookum Jim and Tagish Charley—found a rich vein of the bright yellow metal on Rabbit Creek. In a country where ten cents of gold to the pan was an excellent find, Carmack, Jim and Charley found four dollars to the pan, and the creek was re-named Bonanza.

News of the big find spread like a frantic whisper through the Yukon Valley. All of Bonanza Creek was staked by the end of August, and throughout the winter of 1896-97, hundreds of northerners poured in to set up claims on other creeks.

In June—ten months after the discovery—two ocean-going vessels paused at St. Michael on the Bering Sea—1700 miles west of Dawson—and the first *nouveau riche* Klondike miners boarded the ships. Each with their wealthy cargo, the *Excelsior* was bound for San Francisco and the *Portland* was bound for Seattle. The *Excelsior* was the first vessel to dock at its destination. The word soon-spread: GOLD DISCOVERED IN THE YUKON.

When the *Portland* arrived in Seattle two days later, newsmen and a mad crowd thronged the dock. Miners struggled off the boat under the weight of suitcases well padded with gold, and the people, with a keen sense for sniffing out hidden riches, mobbed them. Seattle police had to use billy sticks to beat off the unruly crowd.

The world was between wars and gold rushes and in need of adventure to stir the imagination. The Yukon gold rush supplied this excitement as men rushed to the wild, forbidding frontier.

Northwest of Carmack's discovery site, at a place

where the Klondike River meets the Yukon, there was a two mile stretch of swamp dotted with tangled willow bushes that flanked the river's edge. It was mosquito-infested in summer and wind-swept and frozen in winter, but here, a pioneer named Joe Ladue, saw an opportunity to make a fortune from the gold rush. He built a saloon at this lonely spot, freighted in lumber and hastily erected shanties. A town began to grow and Ladue called it Dawson City in honor of George M. Dawson, a government geologist.

By the spring of 1897, there were 1500 people in Dawson, but after word spread in Seattle, the town grew into the biggest city west of Winnipeg, with 38,000 people and a gaudy, flamboyant assembly of tents, shanties, log huts, theaters, saloons, gambling dens and churches. The people who swarmed over this frontier were as gaudy and flamboyant as the town—and they shared a common dream...to become rich and famous overnight.

Dawson was in the heart of the gold district—within a 100 mile radius of streams bearing the exotic names of *Pure Gold Creek*, *Gold Bottom*, *Eldorado*, and a mountain called *King Solomon's Dome* from whence these wealthy waters flowed. The district referred to as The Klondike, was as remote and inaccessible as Siberia, and this alone appealed to people who were looking for a challenge. The early fortune seekers who landed there in the fall of 1897, were young, muscular and bold—qualities they needed for the back-breaking climb over mountain passes, for rafting down icy rivers and lakes, and portaging around rapids. The first women, too, were big-boned and brawny; they left boring lives in cities to follow pimps to the gold fields. And when they got there, they were underpaid and isolated in a ghetto-like area across the river called "Lousetown", or consigned to back streets with the ironic names—Paradise Alley and Hell's Half Acre.

Women and nails were among the scarcest items in Dawson by the time that false-fronted dance halls and gambling houses sprang up along the main road. Actresses, vaudeville entertainers and dancers—on their own or hired by burgeoning Dawson establishments—

joined the long line of sweating humanity struggling up the Chilkoot Pass from Dyea, the most popular route into the Klondike.

Cad Wilson—a diminutive red head with expressive brown eyes—was lured to Dawson by Alexander Pantages—a Greek immigrant who had heard about her stage performances in Seattle. It was rumored that Pantages—the owner of *The Orpheum* theater—paid Cad the highest wages ever offered an entertainer in the Pacific Northwest. The miners who packed the dance halls each night loved her song, "Just a Little Lingerie". In a titillating dance number that accompanied the song, she delighted the audience by lifting her skirts high enough to reveal a dazzling diamond garter circling one leg just above the knee.

Cad's lilting contralto voice and appealing stage presence brought a thunderous round of applause from the mottled crowd at *The Orpheum*. Boisterous men threw gold nuggets on stage each time she appeared. One big brute of a miner fell in love with her, and he ordered her tin bath tub at home to be filled with champagne at thirty dollars a pint—a special treat for a special lady. There are no reports to tell whether she bathed in the champagne, but one bartender predicted that whether she did or not, the booze would be salvaged, re-bottled and would go into circulation again.

When Cad left Dawson, after a short ten-month visit, an adoring audience presented her with a parting gift—a belt of gold nuggets that circled her slim waist one and a half times.

A young Greek woman who called herself "The Turkish Whirlwind Danseuse" was fined twenty-five dollars by the North West Mounted Police after she performed a daring number wearing little more than a billowy scarf. It was a hootchie-kootchie dance, performed the year before to raised eyebrows at the world exhibition in Columbia by a dancer known as "Little Egypt". The Mounties considered the dance "obscene" even though the entertainer argued that it was a Mohammedan religious ritual.

In song-dance numbers, entertainers tried to appeal

to men's yearning for home, family and love with such songs as, *"I'll Take You Home Again Kathleen"*, *"Love's Old Sweet Song"*, *"Such a Nice Girl, Too"*, or *"Just Before the Battle Mother"*.

Kitty Rockwell, who became famous as Klondike Kate, had performed on stages in New York City before she went to Dawson with a travelling theater company. A tall, beautiful woman in her early twenties, she told journalists who interviewed her that she was educated in a private convent school in Washington, and her father was a prominent judge there. She often danced in a fifteen hundred dollar Parisian gown covered with rhinestones, and wore a headdress of lighted candles.

Pantages adored her, proposed marriage and she accepted, but at a later date, he went "outside" to crank up his multi-million dollar theater chain, and he married someone else. Kate sued him for breach of promise, asking $25,000—and Pantages settled out of court for a sizeable sum, but she never revealed the amount.

A tinny piano and raspy violin accompanied the dances at theaters with high-sounding names—*Monte Carlo, Tivoli, Orpheum, Palace Grand*. Four short city blocks on Front Street rocked and rolled with all-night entertainment from the dance halls.

Although the outside facades of these buildings differed in their ornate, carved scrollwork and wrought-iron balustrades, they were all alike inside—a small vestibule at the entrance, heated by an iron stove; a long, highly varnished bar at the left where mirrors reflected the bartenders who were dressed in dark trousers, and white waistcoats with diamond stickpins in lapels. Beyond this there was a gaming room, busy night and day with faro, dice, poker and roulette and at the rear of the building the theater came alive at eight o'clock every night (except Sundays) and held performances until the final curtain at seven the next morning.

In these theaters, coal oil lamps in wall brackets, added a mellow glow to the main floor with its rough, movable benches. There was also a balcony, dimly-lit with lamps, where six box seats were reserved for men of afflu-

Klondike Gold Rush Centennial Anthology 71

ence who ordered champagne for themselves and an entourage of beautiful percentage girls. Miners craved the attention that came their way when they were wealthy enough to reserve a box at one of the many theaters. It was a sign that they had "arrived" at the pinnacle of success—wealth and fame.

Many dance hall girls gave up their stage careers for marriage in order to be accepted in the strict, Victorian code of Dawson society. And yet, even with marriage, it was difficult to erase the past—as Gertrude Lovejoy learned. Gertie had come to Dawson as a talented actress, dancer and singer who had performed with well-known theatrical companies in the United States. She gathered enough wealth in gold nuggets tossed at her dainty feet on stage, to buy a large, sparkling diamond, and she paid a dentist to insert the gem between her two front teeth. Dawson loved this touch of glittering eccentricity and called her "Diamond Tooth Gertie". A prominent Dawson lawyer—C.W.C. Taber—fell in love with Gertie, and although reluctant to give up her rewarding stage career to be a wife, she finally accepted his proposal and they were married at a fashionable church wedding in Dawson. Mr. and Mrs. C. W. C. Taber took up residence in the Klondike, but Gertie was never accepted in the homes of upper class citizens because hostesses said her sparkling smile reminded them of her "tarnished" years as an actress.

To be untarnished and respectable, the single woman had to be a virgin and behave like a true puritan. In fact, this code was so entrenched in people's minds, that only in death was one young dance hall girl able to attain her virtue.

Nineteen-year old Myrtle Brocee—a tall, willowy dancer—was wooed by Harry Woolrich, a sallow, taciturn man of fifty-five who operated the gambling concession at the Monte Carlo. He had a room above another casino, and he invited Myrtle to share this room with him. She had been ill with pneumonia, unable to work and was desperate for money and help, so she moved in with Harry. He was not an exciting person to live with. Hooked on gambling, he was constantly away—searching for the big win, and when he got it—a cool $60,000 in a night at roulette—he lost it the next day in a turn of the wheel.

Myrtle and her sister, Florence, performed a song and dance act together at *The Tivoli*—but Myrtle never liked stage life. She told a friend that she disliked being a dance hall girl because, "it brings me the importunities of men."

A few days before her 20th birthday, she shot herself to death in Harry's room. At a coroner's inquest, half a dozen men swore on the Bible that they had shared a bed with the dark-haired beauty, but there had been no sex. Wives of doctors, lawyers, mounties—the Puritanical upper crust of Dawson society—attended Myrtle's funeral, walking to the edge of town to see her buried in perma frost—preserved forever as a virtuous woman.

These early actresses lived and worked where men outnumbered women two hundred to one, and many men became possessive and jealous of sweethearts who earned a living in dance halls. A popular actress at the Monte Carlo—Maud Roselle—was shot to death by her jealous lover, Harry Davis, on a soft summer night in 1899, and later that same summer, a bartender named James Slorah, murdered his girl friend, then turned the gun on himself. He lived, however, stood trial, and served a lifetime in prison for his crime.

Stella Troup—a vivacious nineteen year old—swallowed strychnine and died four days before Christmas.

These young women, along with the young men who struggled to wrest a fortune from the land, lived in a tinsel world where fortunes came and went quickly. The transient quality of this boom and bust life gave them little of substance by which to live.

Some dance hall girls were tougher than others, like The Oregon Mare—a big-boned, tall woman who whistled and whinnied like a horse while dancing. When she walked along the board walk on Front Street, she ordered men to get off so she could float by in her furs or silks— like a lone, reigning queen.

She loved to gamble, and was known to spend a thousand dollars in a single hour at roulette. But—she was also independently wealthy, having struck it rich on a fraction of a claim. She often bellied up to the bar and in a deep, loud voice shouted: "Come have a drink with me, boys—all of you." And with that, she threw her gold poke on the counter to cover expenses.

In the summer of 1898, gold was found at Nome, Alaska, and opportunists left the Klondike to try their luck in a new setting. The Spanish Civil War was also heating up between the United States and Spain, and adventurers left the gold fields to seek excitement and warm beaches in Cuba. By 1899, Dawson was a shadow of her former self, and dance hall girls began to exit. Old theaters closed their doors against a backdrop of memories of a dazzling, deviant, swashbuckling era.

LYNN ROBBINS • CAMP DENNISON, OHIO

Why the Malaspina?

Did they think they'd be able to skate it?
Did they think they could slip-slide up the ice
without effort, without a crevasse or two yawning,
swallowing first the doctor and his chest full of medicine,
then two others, their sleds, their dogs, their yelps
and yells falling deep into white-ice canyons,
no time for tombstones, barely time to pray?

Did they think their tender feet could stand it,
this unlikely band of nineteen from New York,
with unsuited office clerks, a postman, two policemen,
with half a ton of food apiece, setting out in April
up fifty slick miles of glacier, the Malaspina,
the sun burning, blinding, blizzards burying gear,
three months till they came back down to flat earth?

Did they think then that summer would be easy,
that the untouched forests would have paths,
signposts, that the brambles had been cleared,
that a fever (other than gold, and yet the same)
wasn't lurking in the hemlock and dark spruce shadows
ready to claim yet another, or that their pockets
would still be empty, gold only in their teeth?

Or did they think somehow winter would forget to howl
or not sneak up blue-fingered, sending some
running for warm relief, though not all
would make it, vanishing, assumed dead,
while the rest holed up cold until springtime
when death came dressed as scurvy, an avalanche,
starvation as they straggled toward the sea?

And as they perched at the coast by their signal fire,
a hard year since their journey began,
did the four who survived think it worth it?
Did the ones who were snow-blind want their eyes?
Did all of them weep for the lives lost and left there?
And would they, could they, had they, did they
ever stop dreaming of gold?

Klondike Gold Rush Centennial Anthology 75

Kay Boyd, © 1984 · Courtesy of The International Sourdough Reunion

Author Biographies

Joan Rawlins Biggar

Joan Rawlins Biggar grew up in the Northwest Washington Cascades near the locale of pre-Klondike mining activity. As a young schoolteacher, she married construction engineer Robert Biggar and moved to Alaska where they raised their two children.

After returning to Marysville, WA, Joan accompanied Bob to his construction projects and gathered story background. Since her husband s death in 1994, she continues to write, cares for her parents, and enjoys two small granddaughters.

Her magazine credits include personal profiles, poetry and devotional articles, fiction, and historical articles. She is the author of the *Adventure Quest Series* and the *Megan Parnell Mysteries*, both for young adults, and is working on a historical fiction trilogy which includes the Klondike Gold Rush.

Catherine Clark-Sayles

Although originally from West Virginia, I've lived in most of the United States (including leaving my tonsils in Tacoma). I attended college and medical school in Colorado. After a stint in the Army I put down roots in Marin county. I am forty-four and married. I practice internal medicine and geriatrics and write when I can.

Ted Genoways

Ted Genoways is a Henry Hoyns Fellow of Poetry at the University of Virginia and author of *The Dead Have a Way of Returning* (Brooding Heron Press, 1997). His poems have appeared in *DoubleTake*, *New England Review*, *Ploughshares*, and *Prairie Schooner*. He lives in a converted barn on a fifteen acre farm near Earlysville, Virginia, with fiction writer Stanley Williams, playwright Jeanmarie Higgins, naturalist Mary Anne Andrei, and his yellow Labrador retriever, Hadley.

Kate Hutchings Gross

Kate Hutchings Gross is a sixth generation seafarer and writes sea stories with conviction, but her juvenile book, *Sunshine*, won a '97 Washington Press award for fiction. A radio and TV copywriter, she did promotion for the San Diego Zoo, has been a technical editor in oceanography and medicine. She teaches advertising and Careers in Writing.

Jane Guilbault

Jane Guilbault recently completed a master's degree in English from the State University of New York at Brockport. Her essays and poems have appeared in the *Rectangle*, *Salt Hill Journal*, and *Lake Affect* magazine. She lives in Rochester, New York with her husband, Brian, and their newborn son, Russell.

James Gurley

James Gurley has lived in Seattle for the last ten years. Currently, he works as a technical librarian at an aerospace company near Seattle, and is assistant editor of the on-line literary e-zine *Salmon Bay Review*. In 1981 he ws awarded the American Academy of Poets Prize at Wake Forest University. Since then, he has published over thirty poems in Canadian and U.S. literary magazines, including most recently in *Poetry*, *Poetry Northwest*, and *Bloomsbury Review*. He was awarded a 1993 GAP grant from the Washington State Artist Trust, a 1994 research and development grant from the Seattle Arts Commission, and a 1996 special projects grant from the King County Arts Commission. A chapbook of his poems entitled, *Transformations*, was published in 1995.

Bill Miles

Bill Miles has lived in Alaska twenty-five years and is presently a graduate student at the University of Miami aiming for an M.F.A. in creative writing.

Hope Morritt

Hope Morritt worked in Whitehorse for three years. Her book *Land of the Fireweed*, (Alaska Northwest Publishing Co., 1987) is a memoir of those years. Born in Edmonton, Alberta, Morritt is the author of three history books, three novels and a book of poetry, published in the United States, Great Britain and Canada. One of her Yukon stories won first prize in the *Detroit Magazine*'s fiction competition, 1984. She is a member of The Writers' Union of Canada and PEN International.

Lynn Robbins

Lynn Robbins is a freelance graphic designer who has self-published several volumes of poetry and a series of illustrated, inspirational gift books called *Wishes*. Her peotry has won several awards, including third place in the 1997 Poet's Market Poetry Contest.

Christine Schmitz

Christine Schmitz is a former editor for the *Independence Daily Reporter*, Independence, KS. Currently, she is a creative writing teacher and MFA student at the University of Florida. Schmitz' recent accomplishments include winning the 1997 Porter Fellowship for Outstanding Young Writers and being named semi-finalist in the 1997 Discovery/The Nation prize. She resides in Gainesville, FL, with her husband Tony.

John W. Washburn

John Washburn is a former educator and presently owns and operates The Trailhead Wilderness Lodge in the Adirondack Mountains of New York. He is a licensed outdoor guide, storyteller, and interpreter of Robert W. Service. He is a serious student of the Klondike Gold Rush and has made numerous trips to Alaska and the Yukon, including three trips over the Chilkoot Pass. He is currently writing an account of the life of Joseph Ladue, the founder of Dawson City.

Anthony Russell White

Anthony Russell White is a native Texan, but has lived in Northern California since 1954. Previously an art historian, he returned to poetry in 1992. *Southern Poetry Review*, *Coffeehouse*, *Journeymen*, *Everyman*, and *CQ* have published his work, as well as seven group chapbooks. He is the chapbook editor for the SJCPL Asilomar workshops. A personal high point for him was a 1994 visit to the tomb of Jelaluddin Rumi in Konya, Turkey.

Sponsors

In the following pages are listed those individual and corporate sponsors who gave the dollars needed to publish this anthology. We are grateful to them.

Thomas A. and Miriam Alberg

The fathers of Seattle residents *Tom* and *Miriam Alberg* had links with the Klondike Gold Rush. Swedish immigrant *Julius Johansson Alberg* worked in the gold fields of Nome, Alaska in 1899, married *Hilda Dahlquist* and settled in Bellingham, Washington, then worked as a lumber jack until he lost his leg in a train accident. He used his $1800 settlement to go to Pacific Lutheran Academy in Tacoma; graduating in 1908, kept books for a lumber mill before owning his own sawmill operations. In addition to Thomas, they had a daughter, *June Betty (Schultz)* of Renton. *Tom* and *Miriam Alberg* are the parents of *Tom Austin, Michael John, Katie Lynn, David Julius,* and *Anne Marie. June Schultz* has one son, *Michael Roy Schultz.*

Miriam Alberg's father, *Arthur Isaac Twitchell*, was a homesteader from Wolfe Point, Montana who took part in the 1898 Klondike Gold Rush. He married *Jennie Gaslin* and they had five children: *Jessie Austin, Forrest, John, Robert,* and *Miriam.*

Lela Powell, Carol Lee Powell Davis, Sharol Powell Buchanan

Imagine discovering an old worn leather pouch hidden away for a century! My eyes widened and a smile escaped when I found something more valuable than GOLD – the maps, letters, and other documents belonging to my grandfather who was an active participant in the Klondike Gold Rush. *John Conover Powell*, December 15, 1868 to November 10, 1932, graduate of Yale. At twenty-nine his pioneer spirit led him from Ohio to Rampart City, Alaska. Original Klondike claims and his handwritten map in our possession show dates from 1897 through 1899, including creeks with the names of Dawson, Julia, Russian, Hunter, Lenora, Hoosier, Montana, Granite, Big Minook, Grouse and Idaho Bar. The Troy Press, N.Y., Oct 25, 1897 included John C. Powell's account of "The Alaskan Tragedy" and H. B. Tucker's last 'letters of his trip up the Yukon and J. C. Powell's efforts to save him. Also are market orders for the trip on the steamer John H. Healy, inventory lists and Powell's bill for making Tucker's coffin, and retrieving and bringing the body back to Rampart City. Powell was an assessor, conveyer, recorder, miner, and owner of claims, and on the Hospital Committee Treasury in Rampart City. Survived by daughter *Caroline Powell (Westerberg)* still living in Alaska. His sons, *John C. Jr.* and *Thomas E. Powell*, died November 26, 1940 and January 28, 1994 respectively. Also living are wife of *Thomas, Lela May (Dodds) Powell*, granddaughters *Carol Lee Powell (Davis)* and *Sharol Lynn Powell (Buchanan)*; great grandchildren *Brian, Shannon* and *Greg (Davis)* and *Laurie, Tom* and *Molly (Buchanan)*; and great great granddaughters *Zoie Lee (Miller)* and *Alison Lynn (Rohrich)*. This is a real pot of GOLD!

Greater Seattle Chamber of Commerce

In April of 1882, the new Seattle Chamber of Commerce took its first action, supporting a recently granted mail route to Sitka. The contract, threatened by competing interests in Portland, survived, and thus began a tradition of Seattle Chamber leadership in competing for opportunity in the North.

Fifteen years later, the legendary "ton of gold" landed in Seattle, and the Chamber moved quickly to ensure the path to the Klondike included Seattle. The Chamber hired public relations genius Erastus Brainerd, whose skillful work brought eighty percent of the stampeders through Seattle, where they purchased outfits from accommodating (and soon wealthy) local merchants.

Supplying the needs of Alaskans is still big business. Alaska trade brings $3 billion a year and 90,000 jobs to the Puget Sound economy.

While Seattle's location makes it a natural jumping off point for people and supplies, the Chamber has never taken this relationship for granted. The job of the Alaska Committee, the Chamber's oldest and largest committee, is to keep Seattle the gateway to Alaska. Trade that began with fishing and mining has thrived through, oil, timber, tourism and other industries.

The Greater Seattle Chamber of Commerce works to ensure the Alaska connection continues to benefit Seattle area businesses and their customers in the North.

Photo courtesy of the Museum of History and Industry

Seattle businessmen on the 1913 Seattle Chamber Alaska Tour, an event which continues today.

Klondike Gold Rush Centennial Anthology 83

Puget Sound Energy

Gold Fever - Just What the Doctor Ordered

Back in the 1890s Seattle discovered that gold fever can be good for what ails you.

And Seattle was definitely ailing. First, the Great Seattle Fire of 1889 wiped out sixty square blocks of downtown Seattle – including the fledgling gas and electric utilities.Then the Panic of 1893 struck the city a devastating blow. Businesses failed and schools closed because there was no money to pay teachers. People who did have money could buy a seven course dinner with wine for fifty cents. A wool suit cost $3.90.

Four years of frustration ended with a whoop and a holler when the good ship *Portland* arrived in Seattle from the Klondike with its fabled "ton of gold."It was just what Seattle needed to get back on its feet. In the ten years following the gold strike, some 100,000 miners passed through the city, leaving $200 million behind with the business community.

It was just the kind of push Seattle's gas lighting and electric utilities needed. The region had an array of small electric and gas utilities, struggling to serve the needs of a growing population and industrial base. A complete reorganization of the area's utility industry occurred in the late 1800s, consolidating and unifying operations to better serve the region.

By 1904, the Seattle Lighting Company was formed, serving the area primarily with gas lighting and gas-heated water. It eventually changed its name to Seattle Gas Company, which operated a gas plant on the north shore of Lake Union, the site of historic Gasworks Park. When it was possible to bring natural gas to the region in the mid-1950s, a couple of regional energy utilities merged to form Washington Natural Gas.

It wasn't too long after the 1897 gold rush that Seattle Electric Company was formed. It led to the 1912 incorporation of Puget Sound Traction, Light and Power Company, which later became Puget Sound Power and Light Company.

From those humble beginnings, Puget Sound Energy has grown to become Washington state's largest investor-owned utility, providing electric and natural gas service to more than one million homes and businesses.

While our roots go back to around the turn of the last

century, Puget Sound Energy is also one of Pacific Northwest's newest companies. The company was formed by the February 1997 merger of Washington Energy Company, parent of Washington Natural Gas, and Puget Sound Power and Light Company.

Though technology and the range of services we provide have changed greatly since those early years, our basic mission has not – providing safe, reliable and responsive energy services.

Our commitment to help make the communities we serve better places to live and work also remains as steadfast as ever. And so Puget Sound Energy is proud to be a sponsor of the Klondike Gold Rush Centennial Anthology. We salute those whose work is included in this volume and we thank you for this opportunity to once again get in touch with a rich past.

PSE PUGET SOUND ENERGY

Seafirst Bank

In 1870 Seattle pioneer Dexter Horton sold his general store, installed a second-hand safe in a frame building downtown and called it a bank. Dexter Horton & Co., early predecessor of Seafirst Bank, grew throughout the rest of the nineteenth and well into the twentieth century by acquiring smaller community banks across the state, remaining rooted in those communities as deeply as it still is in Seattle. The bank became Seattle-First National Bank in 1935 at the same time that it acquired the Spokane and Eastern Trust Co. Seafirst archives show that in the late nineteenth century the bank financed many of the prospectors who came through Seattle en route to the Alaska Gold Rush, and later handled their gold dust. Never a bank to stand by and watch others do business, throughout its long history Seafirst has helped the city of Seattle and the state of Washington grow and prosper, financing governments, municipalities, industries, real estate, agriculture, and small businesses. Today, more than a million Washington families bank with Seafirst Bank, a division of the Bank of America.

1 SEAFIRST

US WEST

Fifteen years before the Klondike Gold Rush, John Sabin, general manager of the Pacific Bell Telephone Company in San Francisco, asked his private secretary, "How would you like to go to Seattle?"

"Where is Seattle?" came the response. By fall of that year, E.W. Melse, with map in hand, arrived in Seattle to open the first telephone exchange in Washington Territory. It was the fourth telephone exchange to be opened on the West Coast. It was the beginning of US WEST's proud history in Seattle.

Today, US WEST provides a full range of telecommunication services - including wireline, wireless PCS and data networking to more than 25 million customers in fourteen western and midwestern states. Formerly known as Pacific Northwest Bell, the company became part of US WEST in 1984 and has provided high quality phone service continuously for more than 100 years.

The first telephone exchange franchise in Seattle was issued in 1883 to the "Pacific Bell Telephone Company." Construction began at Second Avenue and Cherry Street. The Seattle exchange was allied with the Bell service from its inception and has always been identified with the Bell system.

The Great Seattle Fire of 1889 forced reconstruction of the exchange. At that time, the company had 244 subscribers.

Then, in 1897, tens of thousands of people began streaming north from Seattle on a 1,500 mile journey, gripped by Gold Rush fever. Seattle, "the gateway to the Yukon," was directly in the path of the Klondike stampede and business began booming. With the increase of business and people, expansion of telephone facilities was necessary. In the few years surrounding the Klondike stampede, the number of telephones in use increased tenfold.

Today, US WEST is working to offer customers one-stop shopping with complete integrated solutions and services few could have imagined years ago. Spending more than $4 million per work day to meet service needs and bring new technologies to the market, US WEST **USWEST**®
is continuing its long history of suc-
cess in the Northwest. _life's better here_

Other Sponsors

Steven Blindheim

Sue Borgensgard Blindheim

Kay Boyd

Butterworth Funeral Homes

Jack R. and Barbara Evans

Reed W. and Denise Jarvis

Shorey's Bookstore

Kay Boyd, © 1984 · Courtesy of The International Sourdough Reunion

Jack R. Evans

Contest Director

Jack R. Evans, originally from Wewoka, Oklahoma, has lived in Seattle since 1960. He recently published two books of poetry, *Window In The Sky* and *Seattle Poems*. Evans has written community histories on the Pike Place Market, Renton, Gig Harbor, Bothell, North Bend—Snoqualmie, a book on old Sweden titled *Swedes—From Whence They Came*, and a biography on *Levant K Thompson, Hop King-Banker-Senator*. Mr. Evans spent twenty years as a stockbroker and investment banker. He has engaged in mining and movie activities, co-producing *Christmas Mountain*, a cowboy Christmas film featuring Slim Pickens and Mark Miller.

Works in progress include a book of essays in verse called *Roll Me Over*, a novel titled *Broker Jim*, and three additional local community histories. He is past president of AKCHO (Association of King County Historical Organization) and is a member of the Pacific Northwest Historians Guild, on the board of directors of Washington Poets Association, and a member of The Academy of American Poets.